In The Air

My Journey of Abuse: A Memoir

Jodi Sullivan

In The Air
My Journey of Abuse: A Memoir

Copyright © 2016 Jodi Sullivan

Front Cover Designed by: Joshua Jordan Design

All rights reserved. No parts of this book may be used or produced by any means; graphic, electronic, or mechanical, including photocopying, recording, taping or using any information storage retrieval system without the written permission of the publisher except in the case of brief quotations embodied in critical articles and reviews.

LEG books may be ordered through booksellers or by contacting: Lady Esquire Group, LLC

P.O. Box 790672

Charlotte, NC 28206 www.writeleg.com

1-888-988-4249

Because of the dynamic nature of the internet, any web addresses or links contained in this book may have changed since publication and may no longer be valid. The views expressed in this work are solely those of the author and do not necessarily reflect the views of the publisher, and the publisher hereby disclaims any responsibility for them.

ISBN: 978-0-9903418-8-8 (sc)
ISBN: 978-0-9903418-9-5 (ebk)

The National Domestic Violence Hotline:
1-800-799-SAFE (7233) · 1-800-787-3224 (TTY)

This story is dedicated to:

The battered women of this world—

May you not let your story go this far.

Professor Barbara Weitz:

Thank you for reading this years ago and encouraging me to publish it then.

Roberta Sussman:

Thank you as my friend and as my proofreader.

My husband Douglas Roger Littell:

Thank you for reviving my beliefs in love and spirituality while supporting letting others know this tale of woe.

Prologue
1993

I can feel the air. This is a sudden thing. Feeling, I mean. I'm not really sure what to do with it. Fleeting thoughts of three years that I erased from my head seven years ago have started creeping back into it. Not fast at first. One here, one there. They come like ants do. We always wonder how the hell they made it into the kitchen but, when the sugar gets left out, they always come from somewhere. They always make it in. First one, then a few, then an army. Memories are like that, too—first, just brief flickers, then followed by an onslaught.

And I can feel the air, coming through some invisible crack in the wall that I built around me then, when I was twenty-four. That wall left me pretty numbed out. Cold.

Jodi Sullivan

Isolated. Fake. Since then, for the last seven years, I have walked around in a different self, casting an image that all is well, acting as if life is wonderful, and projecting an optimistic air. Last year, a friend became so aggravated with me that he declared I looked at the world through rose colored glasses, all the while with me knowing this was the biggest mound of bullshit that I had ever mustered up. For the first time in years, I can feel, really feel again, while I'm not so sure that I want to feel anything. I know I don't want to remember those years. That's why I chose to stash those memories away and forget my life from twenty-one to twenty-four. Deep. Real deep. Into the deepest spot of the ocean of memory, wishing for it to be as vast as the sky, which leads to the galaxy and then to the universe. Oh, that achy desire I had then, during the days that followed right after I got the phone call, to just disperse those memories as mere ashes in the air so they would float away and disintegrate in the next rainfall.

Instead, nowadays I can see that memories stay in the head. Sure, they can be buried, just like people can—so deep they no longer exist. At least this can be believed. I did just that seven years ago when all this ended; I buried all the thoughts about the three years before so deep that I couldn't remember any of that time at all. After a few years of an

In the Air

inability to remember anything from then, I believed that these memories had been usurped from my memory for good, and I would never have to see them again as long as I lived. But I know now that memories aren't like dead people. They just get misplaced and, when least expected, they return. Over the last few months, I have had too many glimpses, countless flashbacks. Sometimes my heart stalls when a stark, vivid image from then intrudes my peripheral vision. Each time this has occurred, I tense up and turn quickly, ready for a confrontation, only to see that nothing is there. Perhaps ghosts and spirits do exist after all. Moments like these have happened during meals, in dreams, at work, and at the height of a romance. They float right into my current thoughts from wherever they were buried and act as if they had never disappeared in the first place.

The first encounter came five months ago, over six years after I left Virginia. Last November, I had already been with Mark a couple of months. I had fallen in love with him, true love for the first time. Mark had taught me that men can be soft, compassionate, caring, and soft spoken. But because of my past experiences with Wayne, most of which had been forgotten, I had a wall around me, and this drove Mark crazy. He had too much to drink one night and, while expressing his frustrations about my distance and

Jodi Sullivan

tendency to shut down when upset rather than communicate, he put his fist through the living room wall. My blood ran cold. That's when I started catching these glimpses of Wayne, as if he were right there next to me in the same room, in the air that surrounded me, mixed in with the oxygen I breathed. The first time I saw this image, my heart beat rapidly as adrenaline shot through me so high that, in a state of panic, I gasped for air, certain that I was going to suffocate. Before this, I thought life was complex. But now I can see how simple this is; the past returns when it's ready.

Since I came back to Miami a few months ago, friends who know of me and about me the best have gotten frustrated. They tend to comment on how I'm just not there; I'm far away somewhere—far, far away. I tell them brashly just to deal with it. It is what it is. Then I just slouch away, muttering, "I am who I am. And there's not a damn thing I can do about it." All my friends today do not know the lost identity from a life gone by, still out there somewhere, still in a world of its own, still superseding me, and still disconnected from my present self—still out there somewhere in the air. Nobody I know understands that. Not a soul. That includes me.

I've read a variety of material about these walls, these figurative walls that people like me tend to build

In the Air

around themselves. Professions don't play any role. Scholars talk about these barriers we build, and laymen talk about them, too. Regardless of who we are, the whore on 8th street in Miami or the queen of England, this is something that we all do for the same reason—self-protection. With memories, the best option is to leave the polluted ones where they belong, outside of our heads.

But nothing's perfect, and there's certainly nothing new about that. Doors eventually have to be opened. Inside air gets stuffy in the literal sense, so I guess it gets that way in the figurative sense as well. As life goes on, the polluted air of memories wanders in the head as the doors and windows of life open and close. Or maybe that stinky air slips through the cracks in the walls or up through the pipes. If the ants can make it into the kitchen every time we leave something sweet laying around, then we should understand that memories can visit us, too, whether we want them or not. With time, we forget about the state we were once in; self-protection from not wanting to breathe it and from wanting to believe it's not there—and never was.

What I do now is affected, eternally shadowed, by what I did then. Today I go up and down, up and down, up and down the longitude of my world, still with no idea of where I'm heading—like travelling far too much and never

Jodi Sullivan

making any decision of when or where to stop. Some people tell me that I get so chilled towards them that this makes them uncomfortable. The scary part about this is the fact that I miss these moments altogether unless someone points them out to me. With an erratic attitude running hot and cold, sometimes I just can't pay attention. So I don't. I can't help but wonder how many times the air around me has been like a tornado when all I had believed was that the air was a light breeze. Today, as oblivion dissipates like a mirage, I can see that there is a crucial flaw in holding steadfast to my certainty that believing is half of anything—being wrong.

These snapshots of the past have been coming more and more with each passing day, so I figure there must be a reason. When they come, people around me wonder what's wrong, where I am, and why I'm suddenly so far away. I even start wondering, trying to figure out what was said or what took place, or what I had missed that had stirred the memory. Whenever this happens, a restless agitation overwhelms me, mostly because the memory just seems to fall out of the air somewhere and always feels so heavy.

1
1985

This was new. The outside air was freezing cold. I lay on the bed, wide awake. Wayne snored next to me, and I couldn't decide what rang louder in my head—his snore, the slap, or the apology. My thoughts wandered back over the past two years. Wayne made a living as a marijuana dealer. His house sat right off of the middle of Little Creek Road, the civilian, city street which conveniently connected Gate Two on Hampton Boulevard to Gate Five on Ocean View Avenue of the Norfolk Naval Base. Wayne sold mostly to naval sailors whenever their ships came to port. Since ships always came and went, he never ran out of buyers. I stared at him as he slept, not knowing what to think or feel. The night before, Charlie, Wayne's marijuana supplier, had been busted on a drug run in North Carolina. "Don't worry about it," I had said with a shrug, just trying to make him feel a little better. "You can't do anything." To me, these had just been words of logic, but they sparked something. After I spoke, Wayne wheeled around and backhanded me into the wall.

The news had come late at night but, rather than go to sleep as usual, I sat in my chair for over two hours, completely dumbfounded, listening to the repetition. "I'm sorry, baby. I'm really sorry. I don't know what came over me."

Suddenly, everything around me seemed new. I kept looking around the room I had lived in with Wayne for nearly two years. The slanted walls of the attic that had been converted into a bedroom came to life, making me feel claustrophobic. The rifles hanging in the rack over the bed sneered at me while I stared at the man whom I had shared my life with but no longer knew. I wondered then if I had ever really known him. Yet I thought I did. Together for two years—hell, we should have been married. And times had seemed all right.

As I stared at him while he slept, he was just a stranger to me—some monster out of a fairy tale lying next to me—the same person whom I had looked up to as a protector, someone to take care of me. Protector. I had met the other side—his darker side—and it was new to me. New and scary and it was real damn cold. February in Norfolk. I laid there in the dark, unable to snuggle up to him,

Jodi Sullivan

wondering when the last time was that I only had myself and a blanket to keep warm.

2

Having dozed back off, I jumped on reflex. Wayne had already woken and was softly stroking my back. I jerked away, not awake yet. "Hey, are you okay?"

My eyes adjusted to the morning sunlight, shining in from the other upstairs bedroom's window while my mood adjusted to fit the prior night. "No, Wayne. I'm not okay."

He scowled and pulled away, letting out an exasperated sigh. His muscular arms folded across his chest. "Ah, you're going to be a real bitch about this, aren't you?"

My ears burned in the cold. I clamped my mouth, grinding my teeth to keep from telling him what an asshole I thought he was right then. He could kill me. He was strong and I had learned how much the night before. I took a deep breath and said cautiously, "Listen, I'm the one who ate the wall last night, not you. Give me some time."

"Whatever." His brown eyes rolled in disgust. This coolness in return sliced through me like a honed knife. How

Jodi Sullivan

long would this take? How long would I need to forgive him? Or could I? The time to get up and walk out had already come and gone. And I had stayed.

3

Quick footsteps pattered on the sidewalk behind me. "Hey, kid, wait up, wouldja?" I stopped as the smile crept up on me. Mike, Wayne's younger brother, had recently moved in downstairs and was sleeping on the couch. To me, they were a family circus with two unemployed brothers and their mother, who ignored everybody else in the house. This came easy to her since she hibernated in her bedroom and did little besides watch television. Out of the three, at least Mike had a sense of humor. He caught up with me. "Man, what is it with you lately? You've been acting weird, Jodi. Out of nowhere, you just up and take off. Disappear for an hour or two. What's up?"

The walks had become a ritual, a routine used to categorize and file away constant emotions that I just wasn't used to. Everything seemed surreal around me at home. I'd walk down the spiral staircase and into sudden states of dread. I'd wake up swallowed in a state of hopelessness.

A wave of anger washed over me while taking a shower. So I would walk, almost every day, to do something with the pent up negative energy as it consumed my thinking. I felt like a panic stricken deer staring into the headlights of a barreling eighteen wheeler. I needed the walks, just to question my sanity, because I was still here. I sighed, then looked into Mike's curious eyes. "Mike, when you and Wayne fight, is it ever for a good reason?"

He laughed, shrugging. "Hell, Jodi, everybody argues. Don't you think…"

I cut him off. "I didn't mean argue, Mike. I meant fight."

We both fell silent and kept walking along the two mile curve. Occasionally, Mike would start to say something and then fall back into a pensive state with his thick black eyebrows connected. As we turned the last corner and started to head back towards the house, Mike stopped, ran his hand through his black, curly hair, and then hugged me. "Wayne hit you, didn't he?" I didn't say anything. "C'mon. Answer me."

I sighed, staring at the sidewalk. "Yeah."

"When?"

"Two weeks ago."

Mike's head shook slightly side to side. His curious look had vanished, replaced with concern. "And you're still here."

I shrugged, looking at a crack in the concrete. "Yeah, I'm still here."

As I looked back at him, he tried to smile but couldn't as his head kept moving side to side. "And so you disappear every day for a little while because you are somewhere right now between a little crazy and downright insane."

I scratched a sudden itch on my neck. "Yeah."

Mike gazed back towards the house. His dark eyes narrowed then opened again when he looked back towards me. His soft, matter-of-fact voice slid into my ear like a freight train. "Get out of here."

I protested. "Why? I love him, Mike. I want to work this out."

He started to speak but stopped, taking another long look at the house. He took a deep breath and put his hands on my shoulders. I looked at the house, wondering what he saw in the white boards and maroon trim that I couldn't see. "Look at me," he commanded softly. I turned my head to the hardened, knowing look on his face. "Get out of here. Now. Just do. Wayne's been your lover for two years. But he's been my older brother all my life. Get out. This will only get worse."

Silence draped over us again, and we remained frozen on the sidewalk, as hard as the concrete beneath us and as icy as the thirty-eight degree air that surrounded us. I pushed and pulled Mike's advice around in my head over and over and over again until I could no longer feel my ears in the cold. Words only make sense when they're listened to, and any fool can toss advice aside, even when knowing that it's right. How what we believe steers the choices we make! I closed my eyes, thinking about the days before, deciding I could handle a slip, and considering this could all be worked out. That's what I believed right then, that everything would and had to be fine. "There's something else you need to know, Mike."

"What?"

I shifted, uneasy. "Right now I'm two weeks late. I think I'm pregnant."

He shrugged. "So? Get an abortion."

"I can't. I don't believe in that."

Mike just stood there, looking pissed. "Then miscarry for Christ's sake." I winced from the stab of the wish by a sharp tongue of someone who cared. Anger and disgust burned with a mix of sympathy in Mike's dark eyes as he slightly shook his head again and then gave me another hug.

Eight days later, the miscarriage came with enough blood for any curse. I laid in the hospital, freaked out that it had come so quickly. Was this just coincidence or mind power? I closed my eyes, feeling spooked but safe.

4

The forest swallowed me as I raced into its mouth, a hidden path that I had found on one of my daily walks. Once inside, the overhead branches of old oak trees blocked the neighborhood lights, the stars and the moon. My arms swayed ahead, pushing off and scraping against the oaks as I ran into them. Dead leaves and sticks crunched and cracked under my feet as I strained to listen, hoping to hear no noise behind me. Once I believed that all I could hear was silence, I collapsed in the dark on dead leaves, out of breath.

The heavy breathing beat in my inner ears like bongo drums. I struggled to hold my breath, fearing the sound would give me away. Where was I? How far had I gone into the forest? I figured I was down close to the creek. I had fled to the forest, huge enough to get lost in, and lost was all I felt. Hell, lost didn't matter. Why should it when trying to escape and fearing to be found? I zipped up the winter jacket, feeling colder from the perspiration that had soaked my shirt after resting long enough to cool off. Two a.m. and I was past tired.

The argument had started because my medicine cost thirty dollars. After paying for it, Wayne complained that he was down to the last one hundred dollars, my medicine cost too much, and I hadn't had any seizures as long as he had known me. "No shit," I retorted. "That's because I've taken the medicine."

He shrugged. "After this, you'll have to quit taking it. I don't have the money for it."

To me, the medicine superseded food, water and air. In sheer frustration, I screamed, "Fuck you!"

He gripped my shirt at the chest and yanked me towards him, shaking me. "Don't you get it?' he screamed at me. "I won't have the money for it!"

"I need my medicine!" I screamed back at him.

"Shut the fuck up!" he yelled back, then he slapped me until I fell to the carpet. He headed down the spiral staircase, hollering something I couldn't hear because of the ringing in my head, and as soon as he had left my sight, I darted out the door and down the balcony staircase.

Whistling blew through the trees like a bird in the spring. I wondered if flocks had come too far north already.

Although nearing the end of April, the air seemed still too cold. Then, footsteps lightly snapped the dead twigs nearby and jolted me into sitting up and holding my breath to listen. Wayne never whistles like that. "Jodi?"

I stiffened, then relaxed. "Yeah, Mike."

He appeared like a shadow in a faint trace of moonlight that flickered through the oaks' canopy. "I thought I saw you take off this way. Wayne was too pissed and ranting to notice." He dropped a quilt and a pillow beside me. "Thought you might be needing these tonight. Another late cold front is supposed to be coming through before morning, so it'll be even worse as the night moves on."

I laughed. "I was just starting to feel cold."

As if by reflex, Mike grabbed the front of my jacket and firmly pulled me to my feet. I pulled back in shock, but he jerked me back towards him. He just looked at me for a long minute, then let me go. "Sorry, kid. I know I ought to be gentler with you after what you go through with my brother, but I'm pissed at you. This happens again, and where are you? In the forest. You ought to be at the airport or the train station, maybe Greyhound. Tonight in the woods isn't the answer. This is the second time already. Wayne didn't even hear me. I was heading up the stairs and watched it all through the side door. Neither of you even noticed I was standing there. I watched him slap you seven times. Sorry I couldn't barge in and save your ass, but Wayne's always been bigger and stronger than me. His 170 to my 140 is a lot of weight in a fight, and I just wasn't willing to get whipped right then."

I wrapped the blanket around me. "This wasn't the second time."

Disgust spread across Mike's face. "You mean there's been another time, too?"

"Two," I muttered.

"Four times in three months? Doesn't that tell you something? Jesus, maybe you are nuts after all."

The pitch black sky cast a peace on the forest. No streetlights killed the stars as the wind swayed the oak limbs back and forth, letting an occasional star shine through. The darkness felt good right then, as if it were a part of me. Mike seemed to be an angel, always knowing where to find me, even in the dark. And in that moment, when absurdity seemed to be the norm, I felt as if Mike's voice was someone talking to me right out of Heaven. But I didn't feel like I belonged there; not in Heaven, not yet. "Thanks for the blanket, Mike."

His fingertips slid gently down my cheek. Warmth crept up my arms. His voice soothed my ear, soft like rabbit fur, something I had always liked. "Are you actually going to sleep out here tonight? The whole night?"

"Yeah."

He nodded, pointing to a clear yet covered spot. "Just leave the stuff out here when you go back then. I'll go ahead and plan to pick it up tomorrow for you. And when you run again, just come right back here, and I'll bring it to you again."

"What do you mean—when I run again?"

He smiled, but the sparkle of humor that usually danced in his dark eyes was absent. "Four times in three months? And you're still here? Thinking what? That this is the last time? That it'll all get better? Things aren't over, Jodi. They're just getting started."

5

Just one beer. Just one. Please. That's what he said. Christ, what line had been crossed now? One had led to two. And they were thirty-two ounce beers, so two of those were almost a regular six pack. And now he was asleep. I paced the balcony, listening to the obnoxious snore that reminded me of the countless snores I had heard from different alcoholic family members over the years while growing up. He had promised me the first day we decided to have a relationship that he would not drink just to make me happy. He had even been good about keeping that promise. First drink while the first slap was not that far in the past. Where had everything suddenly gone so wrong?

I sighed as I circled around and around the balcony, trying to dispel some of the nervous energy. I knew this uneasiness from past experiences. Agitation enveloped me, and such edginess had consumed me in my childhood and teenage years, many times coming home to find my mother's car in the driveway when she should have been at work. The grip of anxiety, the just knowing, would overcome me before I even made it to the refrigerator to measure the wine bottle and see if the amount had diminished since the last time I checked. When I was right and the amount of wine had lessened, a wave of despair inevitably followed. The kick in the gut feeling of hope squashed again would then escalate into sheer anxiety because my mother morphed under the influence of alcohol into someone I never felt like I knew, someone who was bitterly mean spirited. Whenever this happened, I wondered where that part of her came from. Hell, maybe I was just jumping too fast and comparing Wayne to my family too quickly. I tried to put myself in his shoes. We had just been sitting around when the phone call came from Bob, an enemy of Wayne's, who had called to let him know about Dora. Bob had stolen Dora away from Wayne about a year or so before I came along—about four years earlier. Dora's body had been found at an old hotel on Ocean View. The funeral would be closed casket because she had somehow managed to stick the barrel of a rifle in her mouth and still pull the trigger.

    I had heard the news and just sat in the brown, leather rocking chair, swaying back and forth, speechless, unable to fathom how she had managed to do such a feat, when Wayne told me that he needed a beer. Just one. He trembled as tears welled in his eyes. Out of pity, I said, "Okay. Just one."

But the two that equaled the six pack were the end result before he passed out, and I was really having a problem handling that along with the gruesome death. I could have overlooked the one beer, but two made me nervous. I had watched Wayne drink the first one, and it had gone way too fast. "Just need it to calm my nerves," he told me, as he finished the first thirty-two ounce bottle. "I feel so much better now." He had drunk the first one as fast as a glass of water after mowing an acre or two on a ninety-five degree humid afternoon. After not drinking at all for two years, this all seemed too quick to me, so I was nervous. And he hadn't requested my okay before walking out the door and across the street to get the second bottle.

I paced the balcony, waiting for Mike. He had gotten a job and it was time for him to be home—past time. I ached to talk to him. Again, everything around me seemed surreal. Just a fantasy. Some dream. All of this could not be happening so fast. I felt like I was just going to wake up and laugh while coming to the realization that I had just been temporarily stuck in a nightmare. Yeah, it's all that easy. Keep saying it's not real and it can't hurt.

Mike pulled in, and I raced down the balcony staircase to meet him in the driveway. He glanced up the side stairs of the balcony to the door leading into the bedroom. I had turned off the lights. "Is Wayne asleep?" he asked.

With Mike home, relief overtook my agitation. "Yeah. Sure is. He's drunk, too."

Mike's eyebrows shot up. "Oh, shit. Why? He stayed sober for quite some time."

I hesitated, then let the news come out. "Dora committed suicide, Mike. They found her body at a hotel on Ocean View."

Mike stepped back as his jaw dropped. His eyes shut for a second as he looked away, reminding me that he had once been Dora's lover, too—before Wayne. My blunt words had cut through him. "You're kidding," he whispered hoarsely, still not wanting to accept the news.

"No. I'm not kidding. Bob called with the news around seven o'clock. Then Wayne ended up getting drunk on two large bottles of Bud."

Mike shook his head and then gave me a sad smile as he tried to act normal. His hand trembled as he touched my shoulder. "Probably took the money out of Mom's purse since he hasn't been able to find another connection since

Charlie got busted. Let's go sit out back." We walked out into the rear of the backyard and sat in the weeds. Even though it still seemed too cold for me, spring was underway. The lawn needed mowing. Mike kicked off his shoes, crossed his legs, and rested his chin in his right hand with the elbow on his knee. "Well, so the next level has been reached. Welcome to door number two. The consumption of alcohol has begun. You are now certain to be in deep shit if you stay here."

"Mike, he hasn't touched me since the night I spent in the forest."

He laughed, making sure that his eyes had mine locked so he could tell if I was really listening. "But now there's alcohol involved. I have to admit that I was pretty damn impressed when he quit drinking for you. He even told me about that, about how, when you guys were first together, you gave him the ultimatum—he could either have you or the booze. No woman had ever managed to do that before. But you didn't know him before then, Jodi. Wayne's an alcoholic. You've just managed somehow to keep him dry for the last two years. You don't even know how much Mom has loved that! Actually, the house has become far more peaceful since you arrived."

"Really?"

"Yeah, really. Now, watch. The first line has now been crossed. You let him drink that beer. Bet you were feeling sorry for him since he and Dora used to be married and they've got a little kid, so you let him have a drink." Mike stopped, gazing into nothing as if he were searching for something from another time during which I was absent.

Feathered weed tips glowed in the moonlight, swaying with the soft, spring breeze. The first year and a half with Wayne had seemed all right, but why I had ended up here in the first place suddenly saturated my thoughts while Mike was quiet. The night from two summers earlier played through my head like a movie. I ran my fingers through the weeds, remembering the incidents that had sent my life reeling in a downward spiral, out of control, until I had landed where I was—with Wayne.

I had been an ambitious, aspiring future attorney. About a month before I met Wayne, at Old Dominion University, I was taking two classes in the first six week summer term, only to find that this seemed like more than full time in a regular semester. Having let too much time pass, I needed to spend the whole day studying the pre-law class so I would be able to catch up the next day in macroeconomics before the midterms. I had arrived at the pharmacy's coffee counter as soon as the door opened. A friend Rose, in her fifth year of the five year nursing program offered at Old Dominion, worked the counter and kept my coffee full all day long as I studied. As the evening approached and she was ready to leave, she poked me out of the midst of a chapter and suggested, "I think you've had enough of that coffee. Why don't you come over to my house for dinner?"

I looked at my watch. Already past five, I had studied for over eight hours and knew that my retention had started to wane. "Yeah, you're right. I need a break. I can always study some more later on tonight."

We had gone to her house and, after eating baked chicken and yellow rice, the seizure had risen. With a history of temporal lobe epilepsy, I had been having seizures for seven years and had only found out what they really were right before I turned eighteen. The medicine Dilantin had worked at first. Once I remembered to take the dosage regularly, I had even gone a year without any seizures and was excited that I would finally be able to drive. However, on the exact day of the one year anniversary, a few months before, in February, and right after my twenty-first birthday, the seizures had started recurring. The seizure at Rose's apartment was the fourth one since the return, and when it finally ended, I sat at the table with anger swelling inside of me. I yelled, "God damn it!"

Rose watched me across the dining room table. She knew my history. "You just had a seizure, didn't you?"

My chest heaved as my fist pounded on the wooden table. "I'd gone a year, Rose, a fucking year! I thought I was finally going to be able to get my driver's license when these damn things started coming back. Jesus!"

"Well, calm down, Jodi. It already happened and you can't change that now."

I didn't listen to her and kept ranting. Anger and frustration overwhelmed me as I screamed at God and Mother Nature and Fate for cursing me so and, as I ranted, suddenly my thoughts and oral presentations of thoughts weren't the same anymore. I became stuck like the needle of an old turntable, skipping on a scratched record and continually trying to repeat a thought that seemed perfectly clear in my head but came out of me differently. Although the intended word later became lost altogether, the word that kept coming out of my mouth instead was "spool," and I had kept repeating it, trying to say the right word only to hear "spool" in its place. I was perplexed, freaking that "spool" kept coming out, especially since I absolutely hated the thought of sewing or threading a needle.

In the Air

Rose suggested, "We better get you home, Jodi. Let's go."

I kept trying to talk, but words kept coming out of my mouth wrong. My apartment was ten minutes away. I felt strange and the world around me just didn't seem right. As we started around the horseshoe curve on which my apartment was located at the very end, my vision split down the middle in a jagged fashion, like a lightning bolt out of a comic strip. Everything I saw though my left eye moved up, and everything I saw through the right eye moved down. I screamed, "Rosie, I'm seeing double!"

She stopped the car. "Come on. We're here. You can get out of the car."

My breathing had become gasps as I tried to find my apartment through my distorted vision. "I live in the next one down, Rosie, on the end."

"We are on the end," she insisted. "This is the last one."

I moved down the sidewalk, trying to reach an entrance that I couldn't really judge on distance when I suddenly just collapsed into a heap, spread across the grass and the sidewalk. I laid there, thinking clearly but unable to move. I thought to make my right arm move. It didn't listen. My face rested against a tree root and I could feel dirt cling to my tongue, which loathed the discomfort of grit. I concluded that this must be death. What a way to go. Next thing I knew, a siren screamed towards me. The ambulance screeched into the yard that became full of neighbors and paramedics. My roommate Stu gave the paramedics my name and told them that I had epilepsy and had just had a grand mal seizure. This information was reiterated by Rosie, along with the fact that I had been studying and in her company all day. I tried to speak, but all that exited my mouth was garble. My thoughts were clear, but my speech was incoherent. As one who had always loved the gift of gab and had lived through public education as the child who talked too much in class, I kept trying to speak while unable to. In that moment, I feared that I would never be able to speak again and make any sense.

Once inside the ambulance, a woman took my blood pressure. "Jesus! Her blood pressure is two-eighty over two hundred." She wheeled around towards me and her face was fire engine red. "What drugs are you on?" she screamed at me. "Tell us what drugs you're on or we aren't going to be able to do anything for you!"

I tried to tell her that I wasn't on any drugs and that I had been drinking coffee and studying all day long, but the only sounds that came out of my mouth were incoherent garble. The paramedic screamed at me during the entire ride down Hampton Boulevard and didn't stop the accusations until other people finally took over inside the emergency room. "Hold your breath," a lady told me, so I did as she pushed an index and middle finger against my juggler vein. I watched the numbers on the machine as my blood pressure dropped. When it lowered, I discovered that I could speak again. Then the blood pressure shot back up and the garble returned. Finally, she pushed my blood pressure down to nineteen over seventeen, near death, after which it stabilized. I had read somewhere that secondary grand mal seizures could occur after any type of lesser seizure. Now I had experienced that knowledge. I sighed, happy to be alive and able to talk even though I was exhausted.

Then the hospital decided to run a CT scan on my brain and a nurse asked me, "Are you allergic to shellfish?"

I shook my head. "I don't think so. I eat clams and shrimp."

She started running natural iodine in my veins, explaining that this helps make distinctions on the CT scan. As she rattled about medical procedure, lightheadedness took over. Suddenly red spots covered me and these progressed into welts all over my body. My fingers doubled in size while the nurse freaked out that I was having an allergic reaction, so she yelled, "Bring some Benadryl NOW!"

The next morning, I awoke to the bright sun glaring straight into my eyes. I sat straight up in bed, greeted by excruciating pain that shot through the back of my head until it enveloped my entire skull. I screamed, burying my head under the pillow to block the sunlight. Soon, I found out that this was a migraine, a typical aftereffect of a grand mal seizure. Early in the afternoon, I saw my mother coming through the door, and relief swept over me. "Hi, Mom."

She didn't respond warmly. Had she been drinking? She didn't give me a hug. She said I would probably be there a few days because of the allergic reaction. The hospital had to make sure the swelling was down before they could discharge me. I ached for a hug and wondered what the hell was wrong with her. Before I could muster up the courage to ask, she said, "Well, I have to go. Ron will be home early today." And out the door she went, leaving me hurt and angry and wondering if all she thought about was what an inconvenience I was as a daughter since I had epilepsy. I felt abandoned.

I hadn't found out until months later that my neurologist had told my mother I was on cocaine that night. I had gone to see him for a follow up a few months after the seizure. This was always a tedious waiting process, usually an hour. While I waited, I read through my file and found the entry concerning my trip to the hospital: "Grand mal seizure triggered by the use of cocaine." When he had finally entered the room I was in, I had gone ballistic on him, yelling "No wonder my mother hasn't spoken to me! You dumbass! Did you run any blood tests before coming to this inept conclusion?" With that, I stormed out the door. I hadn't gone back since. And in between the seizure and the doctor's visit, I had discovered that I could no longer read. Reading was something I had done all my life. I had spent part of my childhood with my grandmother, who taught first grade and had taught me to read long before I started school, but after the seizure, words swam on the page in front of me. Once I even found my body swaying forward towards the page and wondered if this was where the phrase "falling into a book" came from. The end result was I had fallen from the grace of becoming a future lawyer to becoming a drug dealer's girlfriend who couldn't even read the newspaper.

I pushed the memories away and returned to the weeds swaying in the moonlight. "What makes you think things will just get worse, Mike?"

He half shrugged. "They'll start happening together. Beer and abuse. Whiskey and abuse. Bet Wayne will be getting a bottle of Jack Daniels pretty soon up the road, knowing him." Mike gazed into the air, obviously remembering a past time. "And so, are you going to listen to me and get out of here?"

"I don't know."

"You aren't. Damn. You aren't. I can tell. You fool. You sweet, little fool." His hand ran across my back like a soft breeze. He sat up suddenly with the palm of his hand pressed firmly on my chest, easing me backwards. "Let me make love to you, Jodi." He looked towards the house for just a second, then back to me. "You really won't accept the reality of what you're in. You don't want to believe anything I'm telling you. What a strange state of denial! You won't leave. But all you're going to get anymore from Wayne is fucked. Let me make love to you, just this once, so you won't forget what love is and so you won't forget how it feels for someone to be tender with you when Wayne just beats you all the time."

Warmth crept through the dread. "What if he wakes up?"

"He won't." Humor danced in Mike's eyes as his hand softly stroked my inner thigh. "Alcohol after not having any for a couple of years? Goodbye. He's gone for the night. He won't wake up until morning."

In the Air

I nodded. After watching the outcome of too much alcohol consumption for years in my childhood, I knew he was right. As starved for love as I had felt for over three months, the tingling sensation from his soft touch devoured me. His fingers ran gently through my hair as our lips met. I pulled him towards me as I laid down in the tall grass.

6

Wayne hovered over me with his hands against the corners of the rocking chair that he had pushed against the wall. In that instant, I could only think about how ugly he looked when angry—bulged eyes, clenched teeth, and a furrowed brow destroyed his otherwise handsome face. In a rage, this distortion escalated into another form, like a reddened ogre. I was lost. In the midst of his ranting, I tried to think back about what I might have said to trigger this one, but I couldn't figure out what had instigated him, just like some of the other times in the past that had been the same and just as easy to figure out that, whatever the reason, it wasn't anything important. The why had reached the point that it didn't matter anymore.

"I'm the boss around here!" he screamed at me. "Do you understand?" His 170 pounds of muscle compared to my 108 of skin and bones was all I needed to keep my mouth shut. I almost wouldn't mind him yelling if I just knew what had sparked him. Hell, anyone deserves to blow off steam as long as it makes sense. But I was reaching in the air for a reason, checking corners, racking my brain, and not finding anything. I sat rigid in the chair, empty handed of possible causes, watching Wayne yell that he was the boss and turning ugly again, just all of a sudden changing face. Right in front of me, I watched the fairy tale monster come to life. "Do you hear me? I'm the boss around here!"

"Yeah," I muttered, unable to move, afraid to even flinch at his ogre face hanging and scowling over me. "Yeah, Wayne." My even, calm voice replied, even though I wanted to scream. "You're the boss."

"You better believe it!" And his face wasn't even a foot away from mine. As the unsightliness loomed over me, I held my breath. His right hand came off the back of the chair and closed around my throat instead, pinning me to the back of the chair. He didn't know his own strength, but I sure did. I was learning it by the day. I wondered how long I'd be able to go without breathing and could tell I wasn't getting any air as my face started to feel warm, then numb as the room started to fade. Wayne's voice seemed to scream at me from a distance. "I'm the boss around here and you better believe it!"

His grip eased for a second, but his hand was still on my throat. After gasping for air a few seconds, I spurted, "You're hurting me!"

His hand dropped, and his face returned to normal with some faraway look as if he couldn't believe what he had just done, just like I couldn't believe it. But it had happened again, and I sat still in the chair, trying to figure out which was worse—being slapped or strangled—and deciding that they were the same to me. Wayne backed away from the chair, looking at his hands as though they were aliens. "God, I'm so sorry, baby."

His words chilled me like frostbite. They were as empty as air. I ran my hand across my neck, wanting to believe he meant them while knowing they were false. Like lies.

7

Spinning. I had done that a lot as a kid and I was doing it again as an adult—spinning fast with my arms by my side and my feet almost on top of each other, moving quickly until I just couldn't move any faster or stand it any longer, upon which I fell to the ground in the midst of grass and leaves. Blood rushed up through the capillaries in my head to bring oxygen to the brain cells. Even though at a complete stop, the sensation of moving was still there, just like it was supposed to be. That's what spinning was all about—how to create a false sense of movement. Soon, the sensation ended.

I picked myself up off the grass and finished the walk up to the pharmacy coffee shop. I decided to have coffee at the pharmacy and then take my two mile walk later—all for distance, which had become the norm. I had decided to stay as far away as humanly possible without really going anywhere. Boy, I needed a job, just for distance, and getting a job was tough in this town surrounded by water—the Chesapeake Bay on one side and the Atlantic Ocean on the other—with nowhere left to grow.

Inside the pharmacy, I headed to the coffee shop and sat at the counter next to Pat, a middle aged woman whom I had come to know while there in the past, even before hanging out there more just to escape Wayne. "Hey, Pat, how're you doing?"

"Fine, sweetie. How 'bout yourself?"

"I'm okay. Coffee, please," I said to the waitress. "Plenty of cream."

I poured the cream in, stirred the coffee, and turned to find Pat scrutinizing me over the top of her reading glasses. "You're okay, huh?"

"Yeah. Why?"

Her eyebrows shot up and she shrugged, followed by her sarcastic Southern drawl. "Oh, hell. I don't know. It could be those marks on your neck that have me wondering. Don't know why they affect me. Could be how they look like you had fingers glued to your neck. You know, just fingers minus the prints."

A tingle shot through my body with Pat's sharp, down-to-earth tone as I realized that I had been careless. I hadn't paid attention, hadn't thought about it really, and hadn't looked in the mirror since, so I hadn't thought to cover up the marks. But I had an easy out. "I had a bad seizure last night," I lied.

Pat leafed through her newspaper. "Really? You haven't had one of those since I've known you, and that's going on two years."

I shrugged. "Well, that's ended. They're back." Weak. I was weak and so were my words. I started to feel dizzy again, like I had just fallen from the spin and into the grass.

Pat's tone didn't change. "Okay. If you say so. I can't call you a liar. We've been friends too long for me to do that. But I sure can wonder all I want to. Just looks mighty strange to me."

Friends too long. Her words rang like a siren in my head. Hell, she had probably known something was wrong with me for quite a while. She probably just hadn't been able to put her finger on it or hadn't wanted to say anything without more evidence. And now there was plenty of what she had been waiting for—evidence planted on my neck, even if there weren't any fingerprints. And I had been oblivious to her knowing. She had jumped at the opportunity like a stalking cat that had been waiting, waiting patiently

Jodi Sullivan

for quite some time for the mouse to stick its head out of the hole.

I felt chilled. June. It had to be the air conditioning. No sweat. The coffee was hot.

8

Beer and abuse. Whiskey and abuse. Those had been Mike's words of warning. The throat grip was the first time the two had come together. It wasn't always that way. They could happen apart from each other, too. I had seen that for years, growing up. They strengthened each other like two people lifting a piece of furniture instead of one. Together, two people could do much more than two times what each could do alone. The magnitude was not a simple addition process, but more like multiplication. The real problem with the alcohol effect, though, was the numbers. They always varied and were never predictable.

I sat down for a rest at the back turn. I had to. The day was hot and humid, and I was drained of energy with a mile left to go. Between the coffee and the walk, I had only stopped at the house for a few minutes to cool off and get something cold to drink. Wayne hadn't said anything at first. He had just stared at me, then through me. Listless. Then he had stuck his arm in front of me, clinging the door frame, to block my way out. "I don't like the way you leave here all the time."

His voice was low and threatening. No anger or hostility came out, but its coldness struck an inner nerve and my muscles tensed while a tingling spread, as if a swarm of little piss ants were crawling up and down the erect hairs on my arms to meet somewhere on the back of my neck. "I just need the walks," I said quietly. My mouth went dry and I was grateful for the water I held as I swigged a little. "The exercise is good for the heart."

Good for the heart caught in a lie, I thought after he dropped his arm and I headed out the door. Nothing had been the same as it once was. Nothing. Not since the first time, five months back. Not only had he changed, but I had also changed and was just starting to recognize this. My need for distance was everywhere—physical, mental, and emotional. I felt detached more and more with each passing day.

But I still loved him, didn't I? I still tried to be there, to think I belonged there, and to feel the closeness that I had once believed I felt. Isn't that what love is all about? Trying?

Forgiving others for their mistakes and accepting them in spite of their flaws? Or had all of this just been cast aside, just a shattered piece of my soul? Once gone, can it ever really come back? Can it be put back together like a jigsaw puzzle or does it just stay gone forever? Can it be fixed or is it irreparable?

"I heard you fighting again last night."

I jumped. I hadn't even heard the car. I didn't even remember that I was lying in the grass. I hadn't thought to cover up the marks, either, and now Mike was standing over me. The marks screamed like wild animals with no vocal chords. Mike held out his hand and helped me to my feet. No words came out as his fingers ran softly over my neck. I flinched. "It's sore."

"Mmm-hmm." His continual suggestion to get out rung in my head. He looked away from me. "Looks like you had a strangling argument with Wayne last night. You must've choked on your words." He looked back at me, trying to smile with the pun, but he couldn't. "Literally."

"Funny, Mike. I didn't argue with him at all. He was in a rage and I couldn't figure out why. I managed to get myself strangled while keeping my mouth shut."

"And you're still here."

"Yeah."

"And still taking these walks."

I nodded. "Yeah."

"Still." I looked him in the eye. He asked, "What are you waiting for?"

I stood there, confused. As much denial as there was on my part, I knew the reality. Why did I have so much emotional stress? There was a fear there, a strange fear of just letting go. As bad as it was, at least it was something, and something is better than nothing, right? The thought of letting go made me panic, and the thought of staying made me panic, too. Was this the two edged sword that I had always heard about, the catch-22 of love? I shrugged to answer the question. "Thanks again, Mike."

"For what?"

"For just being here."

"No sweat. Hopefully, you'll wake up someday, then where I am won't matter to you anymore. You won't need me anymore when you get around to relying on yourself." He gestured towards the car. "Need a ride?"

Dependent? Was he saying I was dependent? On what? Hell, I didn't drink. My family did—my mother, my grandfather, and just about every great aunt and great uncle in my family tree. Dependent? Was Mike saying that I was like that, too? How could I be if I didn't drink? The occasional joint, the once in a while buzz didn't count. That couldn't be it. Dependent? No, he couldn't have been meaning that. Dependent? Hell, not me.

9

I sensed the commotion, mostly with my ears. Excited whispers travelled inside the door, then dropped about a foot away from me, right before they reached me. But I was picking up the tone and it was different to where I didn't know what to think. Wayne came through the door. Tommy and Richard, a couple of druggies who lived down the street, tagged along behind him. Wayne reached up and slid a piece of wood over in the ceiling, a secret place that I had never known existed. Wayne looked at me and smiled. "Whenever you think you know it all, baby, you find out you don't." I could tell he was only speaking to me because I was the only one in the room who didn't seem to know. He reached into the ceiling and pulled out a box. Needles! Christ, a bunch of them. Brand new and individually sealed in plastic.

Needles! The first wave of shock had passed through, but the second had yet to come. Needles. "So," I asked, "What's the drug, y'all?"

Wayne's smile made me sick. This sure wasn't weed. "Dilaudids."

"What are dilaudids?"

"Tablified morphine."

"Morphine," I mused. "And you shoot it, huh? What does it feel like?"

Wayne set the box of needles on the table and took my hand, looking carefully at my arm. "I'd shoot it right here." I glanced down as he slid his finger along a vein down the side of my left wrist. "Then you'd get a burning sensation up your arm." He skimmed his index finger up my arm to my neck. "Then all of a sudden, that sensation will hit your brain and you'll be history for about twelve hours. You'll be wasted and won't be able to do shit. You'll be tired, but you can't sleep. You'll just sit back so high you'll be stupefied, like an idiot."

"And you get a kick out of that?"

"It's a hell of a high."

"So I get to watch three idiots sit around in a coma?"

Wayne shrugged. "There's plenty. If you want to, you can join us."

I breathed deep, remembering the one time I had smoked a joint after the grand mal seizure, about a week after I was released from the hospital. Stuart's boyfriend Danny had rolled one and brought it with us while we were picking Stuart up from one of her off-campus classes. The high had felt so much like the aura of the seizure that I had a panic attack. Since then, I had not smoked any more marijuana nor done any drugs nor consumed any alcohol, even though everyone around me did and even though I had loved to party before the grand mal seizure. I avoided anything that stirred any memory whatsoever of a night that changed my life; the event that had thrust me into an unknown world. But with what life had become, if I were clear in the state of comatose, then I wouldn't be able to make such associations. Hell, why not? I locked my gaze on the needle, thinking of how life had become so hopeless. On my last walk, that feeling had swept through me. "Okay," I said, wondering who was talking, "I'm in on it. I'll try it." Oh, a great escape! How sweet that sounded! Wayne crushed the pill, diluted it with a few drops of water in a spoon, and then held a lighter underneath the rounded metal, explaining that this separated the morphine from the other unnecessary ingredients in the tablet. He pulled the liquid from its top surface in the spoon until the syringe was full. After he tapped my vein to where it bulged out of my skin, he slid the needle in and the shot the juice into my arm. The burning sensation raced up my arm. I watched the location as it travelled upwards, to my elbow, then my shoulder and then my neck, just as Wayne had said it would, until I was no longer there.

We had shot the morphine around noon, and it was ten p.m. when I recognized the world around me again. Tommy and Richard were spread out on the floor. Wayne laid slumped in his leather rocker. They must have shot larger doses that I did. I spoke to them with no response. They were just there. Had I looked like they did? God, what had I done? Why had I let myself get sucked into this? What line had I crossed now? New. Everything was new to me again. I had just walked over another invisible line on the road of temptation. Shit.

"Psst," made me look up, then smile at Mike as he entered the bedroom. "What's up?" He shook his head and rolled his eyes as he looked around at everyone. "Hell, they probably did a lot. Have they been fun to watch?"

"I just landed myself a little while ago."

Mike threw his arms up, then grabbed my arm and pushed me out the side door and onto the balcony. "You mean you did that shit, too? I can tell what they're on—D's!"

I rubbed my arm, edgy. "Aw, c'mon, Mike," I whined, "What was I supposed to do? Just sit around here all day and watch them? Be bored?" Mike shoving me out the door had me upset. I knew too, though, that he just wanted me out of the room. "Besides, who are you to talk? I know about you shooting drugs in the past. You've told me too many stories."

"So what?" His shrill scream was so high pitched that I knew I had hit a nerve somewhere. "My own stupidity doesn't work for you. It's not your own damn excuse. It's not the answer. Before now, you were a virgin to all of this. That much I do know. And that's what matters here, damn it."

I struggled to speak but had nothing to say. He was right. I had been free of this curse until that needle slid into my vein. A wave of terror gripped my chest. I had really screwed up and suddenly, I feared that I had pushed Mike away and destroyed the haven he provided for me. Engulfed by dread, I fled into the woods, horrified by the thought of being alone, paranoid that Mike wouldn't care or look out for me anymore.

I hit the ground far from the house, deep into the woods. Tackled, I lashed, out of control. Finally pinned, I had no choice but to lay still. I couldn't move. Breaths heaved in and out, quicker than the air supply. "Jesus Christ, calm down."

"I can't," I gasped.

His voice was concerned, soothing. Poor judgement on my part. Fear had come too quickly. "C'mon, calm down." Soft, real soft, like rabbit fur. "Relax. I don't like holding you down like this. I didn't mean to blow up at you and get you upset."

Both sides of my face were wet. "I was just scared."

"Scared of what?"

My voice neared inaudible. "Thought you weren't going to care anymore."

He half-laughed. "Aw, kid, c'mon. Less hope that you'll survive it all, maybe, but I won't quit the caring. I promise."

Promises are made to be broken, as the old saying goes, but some people really do keep them. Again, Michael was looking like an angel to me in the moonlight.

10

I lay in the bathtub, massaging my neck. Slowly. Carefully. The hot water alleviated the pain just a little, just a bit. The touch of fingers helped. Nothing was wrong—seriously, anyway. Thank God. At first, I hadn't known. At first, I had thought something might be broken. And this was all over my walk. I had started out the door only to be harshly pulled back, suddenly under Wayne's grip and feeling caged. "You're staying home today," Wayne's gruff voice ordered me.

I tried to pull away from him, but he tightened his fingers on my arm. "Wayne, come on. Let me go."

"Where do you go?"

"Down the street, around the curve, and back."

"It sure takes you awhile."

I shrugged with a sigh. "No it doesn't. I walk slowly and it's two miles."

He shoved me against the wall. With his forearm pressed against my upper chest, I couldn't move. "So tell me," he demanded, with his face just inches away from mine. "Who do you meet while you're out there? Who do you screw around with?"

"No one." The thought of my one night with Mike flew through, but that was only once and it wasn't on a walk—it was out in the backyard.

He pushed harder. "Tell me who it is."

"No one, Wayne. I walk for time to myself." *And to think straight and feel like I can breathe, too, but I'll keep that part to myself.*

"You've been cold in bed to me."

"Well." My voice was cool, matter-of-fact, and viciously sarcastic all at the same time. "For some reason I've just been having a little difficulty being physically affectionate to someone who treats me like a spare punching bag. Something about that just doesn't strike me as romantic."

Wayne pressed even harder against my chest and then abruptly turned away. He looked back at me sideways. "Here, then. Have some more," he said coldly, followed by a yank of my arm and a swift backhand. Since he was holding me, I didn't move with it. The crack from my neck

Jodi Sullivan

exploded in my ears. He let go, pushing me towards the door. "Go ahead. Take your walk."

I stood frozen for fifteen minutes, afraid to even move. The crack kept ringing in my ears. My fingers moved, then my toes, then my body—almost a miracle. After I returned from the walk, the muscles had tightened down the right side of my neck like a rope full of knots.

Hot water. Jesus in disguise.

11

Mike's words "less hope that you'd survive maybe" recurred in my thoughts over and over again. My neck was stiff. There had been enough shit for two days—too much. The spot left by the prick from the needle clung to my arm like a leech, continually tantalizing me, reminding me continuously of where I had let myself go. A night of sleep on my sore neck had turned it into a mass, some lump, like a fist under my skin with a heart pumping away all on its own.

On my walk, I lingered on the concrete hill under the interstate and became sucked into the drone of the vehicles whizzing overhead. Michael had said less hope that I would survive. Maybe. At twenty-three, I was feeling somewhere close to dead while having a less hope attack. Hope whizzed off. Hope came and went with every car, every truck, and every vehicle above me. Hope came and went until nausea swept through me. I was sick of the word. Sick of hope.

Hell, it hadn't been a week since I was strangled. Drugs. Alcohol. Physical pain. These were all coming quicker now to where one day was blending into the next, and something new would happen before I could stop the reeling from the last time. My hands pressed against the concrete, seeking hope but finding something cold, hard, and rough as sandpaper.

Numb, I couldn't pinch myself. Didn't care to. Is this what death feels like? Frigid? Silent? Just don't care anymore? What's the attitude? What's the mood? Numb. I leaned back on the concrete hill, trying to figure out how I felt, just to realize I could not find my feelings. Emotions were buried deep, very deep within. And on the outside, I could still see me in the mirror, as hardened as the concrete hill under the interstate.

I slipped next to Pat and ordered my coffee. "Hey," I greeted her. My voice was low and cold. I poured in the cream.

Her reddish brown eyes that nearly matched her hair peered at me over her reading glasses. "How's it going, sweetie?"

I eyed the spoon while it stirred the coffee, unable to look at her. I kept my eyes on my coffee as it swirled in the round coffee cup. Although I still felt numb, for some reason my face felt hot. "I lied to you, Pat."

"Well…not exactly," she responded, with the "well" drawled out pretty long. I looked up, surprised. She was scrutinizing me over the top of those reading glasses again. "You were still lying to yourself then, Jodi. That's where the truth begins. You had to quit lying to yourself before you could ever get around to being honest with me."

I sipped my coffee. "Well, it's been going on for a while."

She shrugged and then nodded. "Sure it has. Since February."

"Wait a minute—who told you, Pat?" I wondered if Michael knew her.

"You did. You're the one who told me." A chill crawled through me while she spoke. "Why, you've let me know what's been going on just about every day that you've come in here. Every single day. You've been different every time I see you. You've changed from someone who was pretty outgoing with a wicked sense of humor to someone who is withdrawn, moody, and inattentive. You've gotten worse every time I've seen you and that's almost every day."

Jodi Sullivan

    I shivered, cold, wishing for a blanket while knowing one wouldn't do me any good for the inner arctic breeze. Pat had seen it all, had seen me harden, just like the concrete hill. She had seen this in me before I had seen it in myself. She had seen it every day, had seen the hope whizzing by, coming and going. The coffee tasted bitter while I attempted to use it to ease the inner chill while the weatherman rattled about how beautiful the summer day was out there—warm with no clouds and 90 percent humidity.

12

July 4th—some holiday—Independence Day, an anniversary. Self-created, February 4th was the first time, just a coincidence. Five months exactly. Eight scenes. Or was it nine? Maybe seven. No, just six. Hell, I had been so busy trying to forget that I actually might have left one out or added one or two out of spite. Maybe that's what lost in thought is all about. Maybe thoughts really do get lost. First times don't get lost, though. First times stick pretty well, burned into the brain for keeps, even magnified. Something about the first time comes across as significant for one reason or another, and I was remembering February 4th, July 4th. And this was Independence Day.

I was feeling kind of kooky, remembering the conversation that I had with Mike when he had implied that I was dependent. He hadn't really said this, but I could tell that's what he meant. He had left me feeling insulted that night, but now it was July 4th and I couldn't seem to get my

Jodi Sullivan

mind off of that moment. Dependent? On what? On wanting to believe that love was there? On believing that the relationship between Wayne and me was still alive and everything could get better? On just wanting to believe? Pat had said something like that, too, just like Mike had—something about self-honesty, whatever that was.

    I sighed, trying to shake the thoughts. After all, this was a holiday, a time to celebrate—to celebrate freedom, to revel in independence, to believe it's all there by watching the fireworks above as if they're explosions of battleships in a war, and to believe dreams can come true if we really want them to. Half of reaching independence is the belief that it's there to reach, and believing is half of anything.

13

When I was sixteen, I had gone to a camp in Texas. The best part of camp was tubing the Guadalupe River. We would hop into the large tubes and allow the rush of the river to carry us away. Only God knew where the landing point would be. The largest worry was getting sunburned and that's what we would all be by the time we landed somewhere at sunset.

Wayne's fingers moved softly through my hair, snapping me back into my chair. The river washed away. Damn. I had always loved tubing and the feeling that came along with it—the sense that, other than skin cancer from the sunburn, there wasn't a care in the world. Wayne didn't say anything. He just touched me softly. What was that in his eyes? Curiosity? Concern? Was he changing? Or was I just seeing things? "What's up?" I asked. "You sure are thinking pretty deep about something."

"You, baby." He stood over me. Lately, a positioning like that scared me, but I felt okay. I didn't sense the electricity. I didn't feel the tingle spread across my arms. I didn't feel the muscles tighten across my shoulders and the back of my neck. Instead, I felt warm, strangely safe, as if the protector had returned. I didn't feel nervous or panic stricken or fidgety. "I've been cracked up," he explained, "That's all. I'm sorry. I never meant to hurt you. I just cracked up for a while, after Charlie got busted and Dora killed herself, and you've paid the price for it. You really have."

"Yeah," I agreed. "I have."

"Can you forgive me?"

Time stopped. Everything was real quiet, just like a church. And I thought of all the times as a kid that I knelt in the church to pray. Often, those moments started in the same way. *Father, forgive me for I have sinned.* Was I hearing things? No, this was real, and Wayne's words didn't sound empty or cold or hard. This time, I didn't wonder if he were lying. He sounded like he meant what he said. His voice sounded soft and sincere, something I had not heard in a long time. My hands trembled, and the shaking spread up my arms. Wayne's hands eased me up from the chair and into a hug. He kissed me gently while his fingers caressed my hair. I broke. "Yeah, I can. I can forgive you, Wayne."

And I believed this. I believed what I was saying lock, stock, and barrel. I believed he meant what he said, and I believed I forgave him for his wrongdoings. Since believing is half of anything, then believing both sides of an apology-acceptance mended the rift, sewed the rip, and left me in a state of whole. Complete. And I drifted then. Belief has a river somewhere, and I was on it without a care in the world.

14

Regardless of the reconciliation, I couldn't stop the ritual walk, even in the heat. With next to nothing on and a thermos of cold water to avoid a heat stroke, I took off. Wayne wasn't angry about my walks anymore. Instead, he seemed amused and told me I was out of my frickin' mind to be walking in the sweltering heat, after which he would shrug, snicker, then say, "Enjoy yourself." Mike piped up to Wayne's response one day and offered to come with me, bare-chested in his swim trunks. I would have to accept him shirtless. Mike then told Wayne he ought to come, too. Wayne just laughed. "Two lunatics in the house! You guys can go on and have your own heart attacks. I'm not crazy enough to go for a walk in this one hundred degree humid air."

I felt edgy, and I was right. As soon as we were far enough away from the house, Mike lit into me. "What's going on? I don't like what I see."

In the Air

I shrugged as sweat rolled down my face. "Everything's okay."

Mike echoed, "Everything's okay." This was no question.

"Yeah."

"From where are you dreaming this, Jodi?"

I glanced at Mike. His usual boyish face drew in, making him look much older. I sensed his anger. "Mike, we had a talk a few nights ago. Wayne apologized for cracking up and for me paying the price for his madness. Those were his words." I stopped and turned to face Mike. "Then he asked me to forgive him."

Mike's head shook side to side. "And you did."

"Yeah, I did."

"And you believe it."

"Yeah, I do."

"Damn," came out in a long sigh, "And I thought there was hope."

I opened the thermos for a swig of water and then offered it to Mike. He waved off the gesture. "Mike, this was the first time he's been gentle with me since this all started." More water. Swigging this down my throat was an excuse to think and to get my words right. "He asked for forgiveness. That sure was different."

Mike let out an exasperated sigh. "Well, kid, let me tell you something." Lines formed across his forehead. His anger was real and solid and oddly cold, just like the concrete under the bridge where I had felt no hope. "The onus is on you now. All lovey-dovey. Believe whatever the hell you want. Make sure, though, that you get around to asking yourself if you have really forgiven Wayne. Can you? Honestly? Or are you just lying to yourself—again?" I started to speak, but Mike lifted his hand as a gesture to stop me. "Don't answer me. What you say to me doesn't matter. But answer honestly to yourself."

"Hey," I prompted. "Let's walk."

Mike ignored me. "Just one more thing, kid. Right now you think you can breathe. Wake up and realize the only thing that's going on right now is your head has been pulled above the water you've been drowning in. It'll be pushed back under. You'll see."

"Aw, Mike. Ease up. Give it some time."

"Yeah," Mike said with a bite, "Just what you need." We start walking. "More time. I keep telling you Wayne's been my older brother all my life, but you need more time. Yep. More time to find out you should've listened."

15

I sweltered. Damn bus stop. And the time of day was early afternoon. Peak heat. But I felt good. Real good. I felt great—the best I had felt since right before I met Wayne. I had always felt good when I was in college—before the grand mal seizure. I had always had goals and purposes. That had been two years and two months ago. For the first time since then, I was feeling good, real good, just about myself, just about me.

I had been hired almost instantly at a Shoney's restaurant. The interview had lasted for almost two hours. The formality had ended after the first fifteen minutes. The black lady who interviewed me was Ms. Woodhouse. In contrast to her professional appearance, the interview had ended in a lively conversation about the insanity of the restaurant business. I knew enough about it, having spent much of my childhood with my grandparents, who owned two restaurants in Miami. To work in one and do a good job, well, insanity was part of the job description. Just a little. And I sure had a little of that. Ms. Woodhouse did, too. We had laughed and joked while I filled out the paperwork, and I felt great. Hired at Shoney's in downtown Norfolk. Finally, I had the job I had needed for a long time, real long, since that night in June two summers earlier when I could no longer read to study law.

The fear that had come with the grand mal seizure had died, most of it anyway, after a month or so. I had avoided anything that instigated the fear of a seizure, like the marijuana. And now the paralysis, the feeling that comes with fear, was swept away. Gone. All in an interview. So easy. Proof that life can get better. Everything seemed on an upswing, and I was feeling hope. And I believed it. I felt as if I were reaching out and up. A job, great, a job! Maybe this would be a good reinforcement. Money had been a serious setback ever since Charley's bust in North Carolina. Since Wayne hadn't been able to find another connection, money had been a real problem, and now I had a job.

I stood at the bus stop, sweltering and sticky. From a distance, the bus ambled slowly towards me, lazily crawling down the road—far away but coming my way. I waited, uniform in hand. God, I was hot. The bus door opened. As people exited, the air conditioning blew out the door. I felt great. For once, the thought of being cold didn't bother me.

16

The darkened room loomed ahead of me with the lights off and the door standing wide open. I slipped in quietly and flicked the table light on. In the glow of a low wattage bulb, Wayne snored, sprawled across the bed. I started undressing. My eye caught the trash can, as if I had a knack for stumbling over such things, and three empty, large bottles of Budweiser glared back at me in the dim light. I froze, staring at them. Where had they come from? *The 7-Eleven across the street, dumbass.* The sarcastic self-answer floated in my head. I had been guilty—guilty of supplying—just by not being there and just by being enough of a fool to leave money pretty much available.

What was I supposed to do? Hide the money? That sure wouldn't go over too well. Keep it on me? Sure. Then get pickpocketed at work by the bus boy and end up completely broke. Six months of living without any money between Charlie's bust and finding the job, together with all the slaps and hopeless feelings, had left me feeling strange. Having no money can really turn a life upside down, change it, and rip it apart. I had found that out. The six months had shown me that there are two worlds—the one with money and the one without, and the one without any can hurt in more ways than one.

After taking my shower, something was still there. As refreshed as I felt after washing off the greasy smell of the restaurant, something still had me feeling unclean as if I hadn't scrubbed hard enough. I slipped on a pair of blue jeans and a tee-shirt. Past midnight, probably close to one in the morning, I quietly descended the spiral staircase and stepped into the light of the kitchen to find Mike. I hesitated, scanning him for a few seconds and then sighed. No booze. No drugs. Good. He was straight. "Hey, Mike."

"Hey, kid. How's it going?"

"Okay." I leaned against the doorway, watching while he threw a ham sandwich together. He smiled and then made dramatic faces as if he were starving to death and hadn't eaten for a week or two. As his eyeballs bulged at the sight of the sandwich with his mouth wide open, I laughed. "Listen," I started as he chomped a huge bite out of the corner of the bread, "I'm in the mood to go take a walk. Do you want to eat first and come with me?"

His eyes narrowed. "What's up?"

"Nothing," I lied. "It's just dark out there and I don't want to walk alone."

Mike nodded slightly, biting into his sandwich. "Mmm-hmm." He put the sandwich down on the table. "Fine. If you say so. I believe you. And I'm Jesus Christ. Do you believe me, too?"

"Never mind," I snapped. "I'll go it alone." And out the door I went, faster than a laser beam from some science fiction story.

A quarter mile up the road, Mike caught up and walked next to me. At first we did just that—walk. We stayed quiet all the way to the turn. "There it is," he said, pointing.

Pointing at what, I didn't know. "There's what?"

"A great spot to sit down and rest a minute. I had to catch up with you, Speedy." I sighed but the smile crept up on me, too. He added, "So sit your butt down because I sure am sitting down on mine." He plopped on the grass.

Silence covered us like a security blanket. I waited for Mike to start the conversation, but after a while I could tell he wasn't going to just give it to me anymore—he wasn't going to give me the easy out. I had to do some of the work and that included breaking the silence, one of those missions that sometimes gets tough, like an ink stain, which is something so tough that some people don't even try to try. I groped for a word. Just a word. My mind only provided a mix of emotions and images to where I started feeling desperate for a word to start with. I didn't even care if it made any sense, really. Finally, I found a word, or it found me, and blurted out. "Three!"

"Three what?"

My soft voice masked the mood shift back to the feeling that had swept over me while upstairs—back to the freeze, the stare, the creepy sensation that comes with the knack of just knowing before any evidence has been found. "Three bottles of Budweiser."

Mike laid back on the grass and the silence returned. The sense of desperation had waned, and I no longer felt any urge to break the silence. The anxiety had disappeared. Enough had been said in a few words to make the silence comfortable. They had said a lot and the silence felt warm and safe while it lasted. But it had to end, too, and that's a part of something that feels good—it always ends. "So, Jodi, tell me something."

"What?"

Mike propped his head up on his hand while stretched out in the grass. "When are you going to wise up and get the hell out of Dodge? When I am I going to come home one day and find you just up and disappeared and left this all behind, leaving everybody wondering if you had just been a dream? What more do you need to get smart and get out of here?"

I squirmed, thinking about my mother who had walked out of the hospital room when I needed her the most. Even though I had found the lie the doctor had told her, she still believed them. I closed my eyes, picturing the needle as it slid into the pulsing vein of my arm. A lie had created its own truth down the road somehow. Stars flickered at me from the black sky above me. I muttered, "There's nowhere to go." Yeah, that was it. I had finally pegged it—the feeling that I had nowhere else to exist except where I was. And as bad as everything seemed here, at least it had a feeling to it of being somewhere.

Mike laughed, unaware of the inner ache I had. "Place doesn't matter. Where you end up doesn't matter at all. Not when where you are is where you need to leave."

Place mattered—at least it mattered to me. And maybe that was part of the problem.

17

April blocked my way out of the waitress station. "Jodi, you're really being a bitch today. What's the matter with you?"

I stalled. With a tray of food poised on my fingers, I was stuck on the line in neutral even though my brain was revving like a race car engine. With my feet glued to the reddish brown tile, I stared at April. She didn't look mad—just frustrated. A little worried, maybe. "Sorry, man, I said, "I didn't realize I was having such a side effect on others."

I delivered the food and then lingered in the back room. I was on a slow station, but I didn't really care. I rubbed my face, trying to relax. I probably should have called in. After arguing with Wayne, I should have known that taking a day off would be a wise choice. Fights with Wayne lingered in my head long past the end, almost like watching the same movie over and over again. I sighed. I didn't want to be home, either. Leaving the scene was a viable option, too, and coming to work provided an acceptable excuse to leave. I closed my eyes and rested my head in my hands for a moment of peace and silence. I massaged my forehead, wondering why life was so complicated.

My eyes opened to two Amazons standing next to me, one on each side. "Hey," April said quietly, "I didn't mean to get you upset. Are you okay? You've been someone else other than who we've gotten to know since you walked in here today. We were just starting to know you after three weeks. Then wham! You threw us for a loop."

I laughed. "I got into an argument with my boyfriend last night."

Debbie, the black Amazon, asked, "Over what?"

I shook my head. "Nothing, really."

"Nothing?" They echoed in unison.

I laughed again, wondering if they practiced at this. "He was just drunk, and I was pissed off. That's all."

Debbie looked beyond me to April. "Oh, my God, April. I think she might be another one of our type."

April nodded. "Yep. I got that same impression."

"Type?" I looked back and forth at them. "What do you mean?"

In the Air

Debbie looked eye to eye with me and spoke straight. There was no beating around the bush. "You eat shit," she said, giving April a half nod and look of understanding. "All the time, I bet. You're a pro. I can tell. We're going out for a bite after work. You're coming with us whether you want to or not. Don't use the public bus transportation as your excuse tonight. I'm driving and that means you have a ride home. Right now, though, I'm in a busy station. I'm sure there's a bunch of people looking for me who need refills for their coke or more sugar on their table while we're over here looking out for you and ignoring them. And you have no choice here. You're coming."

Later, we all sat in a twenty-four hour truck stop joint off the interstate, eating breakfast somewhere close to midnight. I had been in too tense a mood to ever get around to eating at work, so I was hungry. And while waiting for my order, I thought about how hungry I was in more ways than one. I could feel a hunger for feelings as if I were suffering from a malnutrition of affection. April bit into a strip of bacon as soon as her plate hit the table. Then she got right to the point. "So, tell us. How much does your lover drink?"

I didn't know how to explain it, really, because Wayne's drinking had never really blown itself out of proportion—nothing like the worst I had seen while growing up surrounded by alcoholics. But I was possessed by that feeling I had, that sick, sick feeling of just knowing—knowing that it just is the way it is and knowing what it can become while knowing that could be next week, next month, or maybe next year. Or perhaps tonight when I made it home. Not knowing when but knowing it would be. How much at this point didn't really matter. The feeling of just knowing. That sick, sick feeling of just knowing and not being able to do a damn thing to stop it from happening. That's what mattered to me. So that's what I said finally. "So, why do you stay then?" Debbie asked me.

I shifted in my seat and looked away, staring out the window at the black sky. "I don't know, y'all. I just don't know."

As we finished the food, I could tell they were just being protective of me and didn't want to scare me off by saying too much too fast during an initial conversation. The topic of talk changed to where we griped about the trivialities of work. I smiled at how easily they had just changed the subject to work when they saw me start to get uncomfortable. I remembered times I had changed a subject to ease someone else's discomfort. Whenever I did that, I talked about the weather. Somehow, with April and Debbie,

In the Air

I felt good and still got their message somewhere above the clouds and between the raindrops of conversation. They had figured out more that they were letting on, and I could tell they knew it for the same reason I did.

Personal experience.

18

"Come on," Wayne tried to rationalize with me. "It's your day off."

Ricky and Tommy sat behind Wayne, staying quiet. Junkies. Damn junkies. Those were enough problems already. Yet there were enough drugs for four people—some more of those Dilaudids, that damn morphine—two high dosage pills that were enough for four people to shoot, all bought with my hard earned cash and without my knowledge or approval. I was pissed. I just wanted right then to spit at them. Two days of hard work sat on the table in the shape of two pills. Two damn Dilaudids that could be flushed down the toilet for all I cared.

I sighed. Black market prices. What a trip. That's like buying something for Fifth Avenue prices for something no better than a cheap department store equal. I looked at Ricky and Tommy. They were involved. They were a part of this. Always low on money. Wonder why. "I don't want any," I snapped. "You guys go ahead. Have fun."

If the tone of a voice could cut, mine sure did right then. Everyone looked disappointed. This didn't go as planned I gathered as they gave side glances to each other with the what-now-look on guilt ridden faces. And out the door I went, stalking furiously up the road, blind in a way. I had anger on the brain, more anger than my eyes could make sense of, along with a tingle crawling over my arms and through my chest. "Damn, wait up, would you?"

I had already reached the concrete bridge, and it seemed like I had just left the house. Mike had grabbed my shoulder to stop me. On reflex, I had jerked away. "What, Mike? What do you want?"

He stepped back. "Not much. Just want to know if you're okay. I heard the upstairs door slam and saw you storm off. You look ready to flip out."

Standing still probably had helped. My vision had started coming back just a little so that I could look at Mike and not just visualize the faces I wanted to bash if only I could. But anger hadn't gone anywhere, and I had so much I didn't know what to do with it. "How the hell do you know?" I screamed. "Get out of my head!"

Silence blanketed us, the type that doesn't feel good, like a hand with its fingers holding me in a death grip. While I looked at Mike and into his dark eyes, so brown they were nearly black, the dancing sparkle that was usually there had disappeared. I couldn't read him. Was he angry? Hurt? Maybe both? I didn't know. And the silence gripped me like an iron hand. Right then I knew. Mike was making a decision. His eyes narrowed in a blank stare, and I just knew he was asking himself if he should quit caring. Paranoia quelled my anger. All I could think then was how scared I had felt that night in the woods three months earlier when a promise had been made. That same degree of fear crept across my chest while he stood there, restraining his feelings and watching me through a hardened face. And then, with a long breath, his face relaxed. He was back to himself and shaking his head. "I wasn't in your head."

I sighed, relieved. "Then how'd you know I was flipping out?"

He hugged me. "Oh, just your face. The way you looked. The way you stormed out the door and up the street. I thought you were going to get hit while crossing the ramp that leads on to the interstate. You didn't even look to cross, and you're lucky that gold Lincoln didn't run you over. You missed it all. I called your name out about six times and you didn't seem to hear any of them. You didn't seem to see or hear anything until I physically made you stop walking. So why don't you tell me, then? Tell me how I know. Or does it all make sense now?"

As serious as it all sounded and as sad as it all seemed, I broke out into a laugh and couldn't stop. I didn't think anything was humorous, but my foolery while trapped in a livid state just struck me as I visualized a gold Lincoln swerving to miss me while I stalked the city sidewalks. And it felt good to know that, while all this happened, somebody cared. And to know that Mike did keep a promise about just that—caring.

19

Betrayal. I was lying in the dark with this strange feeling. Creepy popped in my head when I tried to figure out the word for how I felt. Like for some unrelated reason this had all turned into some horror flick, one of those movies that, while watching, the back of the throat goes dry. And why—that's what's important. This wasn't like Frankenstein or dragon movies where the perpetrator could easily be identified strictly by its distinct and often grotesque characteristics, like Frankenstein's jagged head scar or the fire shooting from the mouth of the dragon. For this, there weren't any noticeable monsters, just human beings that anyone would think ordinary if seen walking down the street. So there were no monsters. Just the reality of truth. Just reality that what is feared can really happen.

Stone drunk, Mike had gotten into an argument with Tommy. What the argument had been about, I didn't really know and couldn't remember. Already. I couldn't even

In the Air

remember what had instigated it. Maybe that's because the reason just didn't matter—not to me, anyway. Fury reddened Mike's cheeks and it was directed at Tommy. As a result, Mike told Wayne about some insult, a quote of words that Tom had supposedly said, about Wayne, months ago. Good for nothing bum or something like that. Wayne had gotten pissed. Hell had come and taken over the whole damn neighborhood.

I had been suddenly trapped, or so it seemed—trapped in one of those creepy, paranoid, out of control, what if sensations that it could have been me. With Mike drunk and pissed and arguing with me, such a scenario might have the same sort of outcome. Betrayal. Betrayal of our conversations or perhaps a betrayal of a night now long past. That night had only been a pleasing memory until this moment. That night out back—the first night Wayne had been drunk and Mike and I had made love out in the back yard. That had only been a pleasing memory to me. Until now.

What might happen? What might happen if Mike got pissed off at me? What if he quit caring, then got mad at me and got drunk? All at the same time? Suddenly, the memories of the back yard had gained an entire new meaning. Mike had betrayed Tom, all because of alcohol and anger. The memory that had once pleased me had an entire new angle. The memory had only been good as fact, as a thought. Yet I knew. As a fact, it could also be one of those scenes—right out of some horror flick, the type that sends cruel sensations through the movie watcher, like an axe down the middle of the head or a butcher knife cutting someone's heart out. They'd all be thinking the same thoughts I do about what makes the moment so damn scary. Because it can really happen. To anybody, including me.

20

I pulled a deep breath and heaved myself up. I didn't have to work. It was Tuesday. I slid down the concrete hill. With the sun going down, I watched goosebumps pop up on my arms. I should have brought a sweater. Nights had been cooling off just enough to need one. Crazy. I had been nothing short of crazy since the neighborhood riot. There had been a lot of unnecessary gunfire and fist fights for three days. Fortunately, no one really got hurt much in the end. All the random bullets ended up damaging were tree limbs and a few windows. And I had gone to work all three days and the next two that followed. Each day as I rode the bus up Granby, I would relish the relief that washed over me as the bus pulled further away from the drama. Finally, the neighborhood had calmed down. But I didn't trust the ceasefire.

At this point, I didn't trust anyone or anything. Neighborhood war. Caused by a betrayal. I needed an out.

I needed to funnel out my thoughts before my head exploded. Work just hadn't been the place for this. Even though Debbie and April sensed something was up, customers had kept us running all week to where we hadn't had any time to talk. Besides, after the incident and the neighborhood war, trust had gained new meaning with me. Rather than just rattle and use my talkative ways, I found I couldn't reach out to just anybody. Coffee time.

"Hi, sweetie. It's been awhile."

I grinned. "Yeah, Pat. The job is killing how much we see each other anymore. We ought to come by here before I go to work each day."

"Mmm-hmm. Something's up." She sipped her coffee and set the cup back on the saucer. "I can see well. Even though I don't see you every day, I can see stress all over your face. Has it started again?"

I stirred my coffee and took a swig. "No, Pat. Actually, it's all been pretty calm, at least in the physical abuse category since the middle of June. That's getting close to four months now. But there's something else. Just something. I've kept this secret for a long time, but it's bothering me right now."

"Uh-oh. I don't like the tone of your voice. Go ahead, sweetie. I'm all ears. Shoot."

In the Air

Confiding. Sometimes that is difficult to do. Sometimes there are secrets that shouldn't be told to a best friend. For me, that was Pat, even though she was old enough to be my mother. We had drunk coffee and laughed enough times over two years that no one else knew me as well as she did. I took the risk, knowing that I was safe. Not everyone is that lucky. I told her about the betrayal and the neighborhood war. That sudden sense of dread had enveloped me. Petrified. All because of that one night out in the backyard. That one night I had spent with Mike had just been a pleasant memory, suddenly recurring in a new light. I could only wonder, caught up in the what-if-syndrome. I sighed. "Now I can't help but wonder what the hell is going to happen the day Mike gets mad at me and gets drunk."

Pat pushed her glasses up her nose, then looked at me over the top of the rims anyway. "You've got this all turned upside down, like the afternoon soap operas. Hmm. You want my opinion, right?"

I nodded. "Yeah."

She suggested, "Go to work one day and just don't come home. Catch an airplane. Then land in Jamaica."

I laughed. "Jamaica? Why Jamaica?"

She shrugged and rolled her eyes. "Hell, Puerto Rico. California. Montreal. Doesn't matter. Anywhere. Anywhere, really. But as far away from here as you can get."

"Leave, then?"

Her right index finger poked my forehead. "Well, duh! Jodi, you are already in a damned if you do, damned if you don't, no win situation. Take all that and picture it like it's all one room. This fling you're talking about is like flammable gas leaking in. Now, the way Mike betrayed Tom is like a spare match laying around. Do you really want to stay in that room, knowing a spark can light the match at any time? Tomorrow? Next week? Next year? You're the one in the room. Do you want to be there the day it blows up? Think about it. It's already a shitty place to begin with because of what you've been going through with Wayne, and that's leaving out the leaking gas and the match."

I sighed. "Why is this all so hard?"

Pat half laughed. "Only because you make it hard. Or let it be hard. This seems easy enough to me."

Make it hard, make it complicated. The room of damnation exists because I let myself be there. I had chosen and kept choosing to stay, all the way back to February. All the way back to when the abuse had first started with a slap.

In the Air

The time to leave had come and gone then, and I had stayed. I had made a conscious decision to stay.

Since that night, I had made the same decision, over and over again. After slaps. After drugs. After alcohol. And after the fear of betrayal. All tied together in some perverted way, directly held together by the fear of letting go and the fear of having nothing. As bad as this was, it still felt like I had something. Interrelated decisions tied haphazardly together like a knot that held me fastened into place. So I stayed in that room that was ready to explode while knowing it was a pretty shitty place.

21

Again. It was all happening again, and it was happening too much. No longer was it just a large bottle of Budweiser from the 7-Eleven across the street. Forget beer. Instead, the spirits had turned into fifths of Jack Daniels. A little of that JD. My chest tightened just at the sight of the black labeled bottle, a mean whiskey—real mean because the effect is a lot more intense while so much less is needed. I had seen that, too. My family had shown me plenty of that—for years, for all my life, as long as I had been on planet Earth. In those childhood years, I had seen plenty of JD and a lot of fights. My earliest vivid memory, age two: Mom stumbled through the door drunk, long past the time she was supposed to be home. Dad, agitated, had paced the floor countless times before she arrived, swearing that he would not put up with this. The fight broke out instantly, and Dad slapped Mom, knocking her to the floor. I had stormed across the room, stood between them, folded my arms across my chest, and

In the Air

screamed, "Don't you hit my mommy!" A year later, after my parents divorced, I stayed with my mother's parents. Papa, late getting home, stumbled in, and Nana started screaming at him. Her high pitched voice jolted me from my slumber. I sat straight up on the couch, petrified, and watched Nana sling a large, glass ashtray across the room, barely missing Papa's head. No wonder just the thought of such a drink turned my stomach upside down and made me sick.

While looped on JD, Wayne had started to make some assertion. He had spoken out about being the boss, just like that other time where he had kept it going to the point that he became so ugly. But this time, the alcohol wasn't just beer—it was whiskey, the good old JD. And he tripped right over his own feet and crashed towards the floor, so drunk he couldn't pick himself up. So I laughed, then laughed harder. The bed had no frame, so I finally decided to just leave him lying there in a contorted twist, with one leg under the other in too wide of an angle, his torso partially on the floor while partially on the mattress, and his head wedged between the mattress and the nightstand. I didn't even try to straighten him out or pull away the nightstand so he could fall into a better position. No chance of a pillow for comfort. I left the room, hoping that he would wake up sore.

I hoped that the morning would come with pain for sleeping in such a weird position. Walking out the door, I thought about turning around to spit on him. And I almost did since I could have gotten away with it. I really wanted to, just out of disgust. He wouldn't feel anything. He was out cold. I took a deep breath and swallowed my spite. The evil glee of temptation whispered "But he won't know!" into my ear. As good as it sounded, I knew it was only spite. I liked to believe I didn't need to go that far. So rather than do it, I walked out the door.

In the dark, I sat on the balcony and watched cars occasionally fly by on Little Creek Road. I had left work early that night. For what? Just this. An alcoholic sprawled out in the bedroom, intoxicated, and wedged in a weird position. Hell, he had probably fallen asleep before he landed. Mike's car turned off of Little Creek and into the driveway. I slithered to the back rail, hoping that he wouldn't see me. But he did. So he parked and walked up the balcony's staircase. "Hey, kid. How're you doing?"

"Fine" I snapped, like a cornered wolf.

He walked slowly across the balcony. "You sure are acting strange. Has Wayne started hurting you again?"

"No. It's been awhile."

"Has he been drinking?"

"Yeah. Sure has. JD."

"Right now?"

I laughed. "He's gone."

Mike sat down in one of the patio lounge chairs. He sipped on a Pepsi and watched me for a long time. I felt edgy. All I could think about was the neighborhood war and my conversation with Pat. My fingers drummed the railing whenever I rested from pacing back and forth on the balcony. I moved along the outer edge, just out of Mike's reach. He finally said "Something is really bothering you."

"Don't worry. I'm fine."

I felt backed right into the balcony's corner. Trapped, it seemed, by Mike. And I felt like the wolf, ready to leap and ready to bite. "You aren't fine," Mike responded quietly. "You're going out of your head. You've been pacing in front of me like a lunatic. What has Wayne done to you?"

"Nothing."

His eyebrows furrowed. "Why are you lying to me?"

I faced him and said coldly, "I'm not lying, Mike."

"Then tell me what's wrong, would you? You have me worried." He reached out to touch me, and I pushed him away. Hard. "What the hell was that for, Jodi?"

"Just don't touch me!" I snapped.

Mike's head pulled back as he looked at me. "Don't touch you?" Silence took over, just for a minute. Mike looked confused as he watched me, closely studying my face. I am terrible at hiding anything. I just can't. My face always gives me away, especially when I don't want it to do so. The bewilderment left Mike's face, and he said, "You're mad at me, aren't you?" I didn't answer. I couldn't. "Damn. You are. Why?"

"It doesn't matter."

He disagreed. "Yes it does. It matters to me. Because you matter to me. Come on, let's take a walk. You can be pissed off all you want at me, but at least give me the privilege of knowing why you are." We started walking. When we sat down for a break along the curve, I still hadn't spoken. I didn't feel scared. Privilege. That's what he had said—give him the privilege. Most people would have claimed a right to know. The way he had said privilege made me feel strange. Out of the ordinary in a good way. "Okay," he started when we stopped to take a break. "Please tell me what's up. What have I done that has you so upset?"

I shut my eyes, visualizing the fight with Tom that had led to the neighborhood war the week before, a war just over something that had been said six months ago. The thought of what that could mean just scared me. Like a horror flick. The thought of betrayal had me walking around in circles, in a constant state of fear. I could only think about Mike telling Wayne about the one time we made love in the backyard. I ended with, "I'm scared to trust you now."

Silence met me as Mike thought through what I had said. Then he said softly, "I understand, Jodi. I can understand the association you're making. But betraying Tom is not the same thing as betraying you."

"Betrayal is betrayal, Mike."

"No it isn't. Not really. Think about it. What I did to Tom is missing two things. Two important factors that would make betraying you so much different. First, I don't like or love Tom enough to care about whether or not I protect him. Second, if I betrayed you here, I also would be betraying myself. The only setback that could have gotten me in any trouble with Wayne when it comes to Tom is just the fact that I didn't tell him much sooner. Ha! Wayne didn't even think of that because he was so mad at Tom. Personally, I actually agreed with Tom, but I don't say things like that out loud. I just think them. I've seen Wayne in circumstances far worse than just being a good for nothing bum, and I choose to keep those memories to myself. Betrayal is not just a flat line—it has many levels. So don't worry. Don't make the mistake of associating unrelated topics."

I felt better, realizing that he was right. After all, like he had told me, he had known Wayne for all his life. And suddenly I felt silly for feeling so scared. If Mike betrayed me, then he would betray himself as well. And if anyone knew better than to betray someone and get Wayne pissed because it might include the betrayer, too, that was Mike. In fact, he had known this much longer than I had. He had known it all his life.

22

Cover Girl had covered up the bruise and swelling that still burned. Funny how well the makeup and the act go together. So maybe that's why makeup is for women in the first place. Men sure aren't the ones who get slapped around. Not in the soap operas, not in the movies, and not in real life, either. So they don't need the makeup. They don't need to cover up evidence and hide the burning sensations that stay or hide the marks. And I was tired, just tired of trying to cover up. But I did it anyway, strictly out of habit. Covering up had become the norm, my norm. As routine as brushing my teeth in the morning.

"Are you running a fever or something?" I looked up to see April standing next to me, a large tray of steaming hot food-to-deliver poised on her fingertips. Yet while steam swirled into the air, she was giving me priority and that really made me feel good.

But then I felt a little guilty because food gets cold pretty fast. "No. I'm okay. I'm not sick." The smile hurt, but I let it happen anyway. "Run that food before it freezes. You're standing under an A/C vent."

The amazon cornered me a few minutes later, acting like the act was not intentional. And there we stood, back to talking about trivia. For the moment. "Hey, we close tonight. You, me, and Sue." But Sue didn't matter—she wasn't the aim. Before I realized it, I was conned right into going out for a bite after work.

We sat at the twenty four hour joint and just stayed quiet for a long time, sipping on Coca-Cola and counting our tips. After being conned into coming and knowing it, I didn't have a lot to say. The food came, and we dug in. April pushed her plate aside, finished, while I still had half a tuna sandwich. "Okay, so you got into another argument," she started. "I could tell. You really had your mind somewhere else tonight. You spent the whole shift about a half step behind. All night. You seemed kind of disoriented, like you were half at work and half somewhere else."

I stopped while my teeth were sunk into the tuna sandwich. I sat back and started to chew slowly, then swallow. "Really? Was I that bad?"

She shrugged. "Count your tips. We just had a steady night. What you have should be pretty good."

I dropped the sandwich, suddenly not hungry. I already knew my tips. They weren't extremely bad, but they sure weren't normal, either. And definitely not as good as they should be on a steady night. "Ah, shit."

"Listen," April sighed. She leaned back and propped her feet up. "You, me, and Debbie. We all have one thing in common, Jodi, and that's living with an alcoholic. Debbie and I have both left behind our situations, but you haven't. And you and I have another thing in common, something that Debbie didn't go through."

I felt the inner chill again and shivered. I looked around for the A/C vent but then realized it was too chilly outside. If anything was on right now, it was the heat. "Okay. What do we have in common, April?"

"Physical abuse." She stared straight at me. "It does something to your self-esteem. Something way beyond the alcohol." Her gaze moved out the window to something in the distance. "Besides, I can see what you're hiding. Pretty well, too. Makeup and all." I started to speak, but she cut me off. "I already know what you're going to ask. How could I tell? Well, I'll tell you how. Because one side of your face is swollen from the blow you got last night, the one you are trying to hide. You have it covered pretty well. Hell, I know why you do it. I did it, too. You don't want others to know, almost like you want to protect the guilty. You're a pro at hiding the evidence. Most people don't notice. In fact, only a few do. Your best friend, maybe. And then there are people like me. I've been where you are, and when I see what I see right now, I get the creeps. I feel like I'm looking in the mirror when I look at you."

I sighed. I shouldn't let reality spoil my appetite. I finished the sandwich. "Yeah, it was last night. As usual, over nothing."

"Over nothing like always."

"Yeah."

"Plan on leaving soon?" April asked.

"Been tossing that around since this all started."

"When? When did it all start?"

I shrugged. "Eight months ago. Close to nine."

A sad smile crept across April's face. "It took me three years," she reminisced. "Do me a real big favor."

"What?"

She sighed. "Don't take as long as I did."

23

At one-thirty a.m., April dropped me off in the driveway. The house was dark. I quietly climbed the balcony steps. Inside, I slipped off my clothes without turning on the light. I didn't need it. I had walked around this room so much in two years, I could handle going blind. And then I knew. I knew already in the pitch black room. Some keen awareness had tuned me in to the smell of whiskey that floated in the air of the room. I didn't need any light to see it, and I didn't want to stir the monster. I just wanted to rest, knowing I was nowhere close to the end of my dark fairy tale.

    I moved quietly downstairs, then relaxed in the bathtub. I gently rinsed the makeup off. This time, I looked closely at the finger imprints and a bruise under my left eye. And yeah, just like April had pointed out, the left side was just a touch bigger than the right. Swollen, just big enough to notice if someone knows how to see such minor differences once the makeup is on. Or if they're a best friend, when someone like me has one. I felt lucky. I had Pat. She knew. She had known longer than she let on. She was more than twice my age, close to fifty. Age. I think that's what made it lucky for me to have Pat. That's probably why she could see what I hid, like the swells. But she knew more than others. She knew my ins and outs. She knew my moods. Younger people like me would often shrug off the moodiness, assuming it was just PMS. Short-sighted, easy explanations. The bruise shined, as small as it was, nearing purple. Cover Girl probably wouldn't be enough to cover it up in the morning.

"Hey, wake up," I kept whispering while occasionally shaking Mike. The dream must have been good because he was sleeping deeply. But I had that feeling again, that restless feeling of just wanting to vent out my frustrations to someone who understood, to someone who cared. "Hey, Mike, wake up."

He groaned. His eyes opened, but I could tell he was only half there, probably suffering from whatever he had been doing the night before while he wasn't home. He hadn't been there when Wayne hit me. He didn't even know about it yet. He finally realized it was the middle of the night, and I was sitting next to him. "Hey, kid. What's up? What time is it?"

"Two a.m."

He yawned. "Why the hell are you waking me up?"

"You weren't home last night."

"So?"

"It happened again, Mike."

Mike sat in a stupor for a few seconds, looking confused, trying to figure out what the "it" was. And it took a few seconds. Just a few. And then he knew. He sat up straight, suddenly wide awake. His eyes bulged out of his head. They looked dark. "Ah, fuck. You've got to be kidding me."

"No."

He sighed while patting my shoulder. "I didn't mean that literally, Jodi. It's just that it's been awhile. A long while. I was starting to think he was coming around. What was it over? What did you get into a fight about?"

My eyes rolled then stared at the carpet. "Nothing. Like always, it was over nothing that mattered. I think he creates reasons to get mad just so he can justify having a drink."

Mike led me into the bathroom and looked at the swell and bruise under the left eye. "How many times were you hit?"

"Just one."

"Wow!" He yawned again. I could tell he was tired enough to go back to sleep. "Put your shoes on," he said. "Let's go for a walk." He stopped me as I started to fetch my shoes and gave me a hug. And then a careful, gentle kiss. Right below the damaged eye, where it hurt. He was hoping, I guess, that would make it feel a little better. And wanting to believe it. Believing is half of anything. To me, it felt better, at least on the inside.

Out of the house, we walked to the curve and sat in the same spot we usually did. This had become a ritual within a ritual. "Damn," he started. "Four months. It's been four months since the last time. Even I was starting to think it was over. I thought there was hope." He smiled at me. Then his smile faded as he ran his fingers gently over the swollen area.

My eyes burned with tears. "Mike, that hurts."

He pulled his hand away. "Man, I hate to say this, but I told you so. I told you this was going to happen, a few days after you and Wayne made up. I told you that it wasn't going to work. I told you that he'd push your head back under the water again. And the night I made love to you, I told you all you were going to get from him is fucked. And still. Still you walk around in self-denial—trying to change the reality that isn't going to change." He eased me back, telling me to relax and not to worry—he wouldn't bite. "You really need to get out of here. Christ, I sound like a broken record."

I changed the subject. "Mike, where do you go?"

"What do you mean?"

I shrugged. "I mean just that. Where do you go? Sometimes you're not at home. Like last night, or the time all the drugs were bought with my money. You weren't home that night, either. So where are you?"

"What's wrong?" He grinned. A sparkle danced in his dark eyes. "Hey, are you jealous?"

"Jealous? No—"

"Get out of here! You are!"

"Well—"

"Jesus. You're maintaining a crappy relationship with my brother, who treats you like shit, and now falling in love with me, too?"

Sulkiness enveloped me. "So who says you can't love two people at the same time?"

He laughed. "Ah, don't. Jodi, don't. Please." He got serious even though he couldn't help smiling. "Let me tell you where I go. Let me tell you, then use this information to make some wise decisions. First, I haven't made love to anybody since the night I made love to you out in the backyard. But second, I drink. I drink and I get mean, real fucking mean, just like Wayne. You should know that already, from that one night I did come home after my fight with Tom. And with what's gone on around here, I promised myself I wouldn't come home drunk anymore because you put up with enough shit around here already. So sometimes I sleep over at Ricky's house when I'm plastered." He half laughed. "A couple of times I've crashed out in the woods just to stay out of here. And there's more."

I wasn't sure I wanted to know, but I asked anyway. "What?"

He stared into the distance, through the window of the past. "I almost slapped Dora once. It was only once and it was only an almost. Not real. Not like Wayne really hits you. But the memory scares me. And it's the main reason I don't come home when I'm drunk. The last thing you need is two nut jobs at the same time. And I get worried because I know I can reach that point. I've been there."

"But, Mike," I protested. "You didn't do it—right?"

"No,' he agreed, "I didn't." And he stared into space again, as if looking at the past a little longer would make it come through more clearly. "I just remember it was over nothing. I had come home drunk so late it was early morning, and Dora had gotten up to go to work, and while she was getting ready, the radio was on and playing a little too loud for my headache. So, the urge was over nothing. I almost lost it over nothing. Just like Wayne does with you. That shows me that I'm capable. Hell, I already know how crazy I can get when there is a good reason." He kissed me below the eye again. I smiled, even though it hurt, appreciating what he had said. Most people would have left such thoughts swept under the rug, like old dust. Why was he so honest with me? It didn't matter. I felt okay, at least for the moment, with him, even though his honesty had exposed his own monster. Mike had revealed that he was just a mirrored image of his older brother. Hell, no wonder he knew Wayne so well. They had a lot in common.

24

Just a small party and near midnight on Halloween with ghosts, goblins and other creatures. And horror flicks. The type that last forever. And, boy, did the last nine months sure feel like a dance with eternity. I reflected back to when this all had started. Remembering the miscarriage, I shuddered. I could have been holding a baby, between a month and two months old. How spooked I had felt then, that night in the hospital. A witch raced by on a broom, cackling at me. I smiled back at her even though I mused that I had been experiencing a Halloween of my own all year long. A baby on top of it? That would have been a real scare.

Head games—not fun to play, and here I was, doing it to myself again. Halloween. Ghosts, goblins and monsters, maybe from fairy tales. Hell, I didn't know. I didn't know where they were coming from or who they

In the Air

were, but everyone caught in the Halloween spirit acted amused, pretended to be spooked, Spooked. All as one big joke. Just spooked in some twisted sense of humor.

This was done all the time, every year, by countless people. This act of being spooked was a downright tradition, like it was funny, a part of a comedy rather than the opposite—a tragedy. And I felt like asking. I sat apart from everyone with a yearning to ask. Hey, do you know what it feels like? Do you know? Do you ever stop to wonder? About the real goblins in real life? The ones that let you in? The ones that haunt your life every single day? The ones you don't seek the exorcist for? The ones that seem like normal people when you pass them on the street? These monsters just stay and haunt and work on the sanity of whoever the victim happens to be. Sanity wears away a little at a time. So have you ever been the victim? The victim of being haunted?

This is all there, in horror flicks and in Halloween. I tried to stay in a good mood, be caught up in the festival atmosphere. But the head games got to me, and I was drained. Everyone else was just getting started with the party. I apologized for wimping out on everybody. A hard day at work, I whined. What a lie! Another one of those goblins in life. I went upstairs and turned out the lights. I

Jodi Sullivan

turned on the radio, looking for some soft music to help me go to sleep. But I knew it didn't matter what the music ended up being. I was wide awake.

25

I zipped up my jacket, getting ready for a walk so I could see Pat. To have more time to talk, we had gotten into a reversal and met for coffee in the morning since I had to work in the afternoon and evening. And I was going early, as early as I could. I hadn't been awake five minutes. And the cold front sure had changed the temperature from the low seventies to the mid-forties. Suited me fine. I was getting that ice in my blood. Again.

Wayne watched me, but I knew I was okay for the moment. If he had wanted to stop me this time, he would have already done so. His assertion would have already happened, and I knew it was past that point. Sort of an intuitive knack. The just knowing. I had a talent for that. I opened the door to the patio, met by a blast of cold, heavy air, right in the face. "Let me ask you something," he demanded.

I turned slowly in the doorway, looking back. It hadn't even been a damn week. Not even seven measly days.

And I wasn't putting on makeup this time. I didn't care who saw. It hurt too much to wash it off. That's what mattered the most—to me. "What, Wayne? What do you want to know?"

"How many people have you told?"

I stood in the doorway, staring at him. And the cold air didn't even phase me. Anger built furiously, like a volcano. The heat rushed up my neck to my ears. I was ready to blow and let the lava flow. With a deep breath, I stuffed it away, stuffed it below the snow on the mountaintop. "Fuck you, Wayne. I haven't told anybody. Not a soul. So fuck you. But the next time you want to know how many people know about it, ask the right fucking question. Ask me how many people have told me they know. Ask me that question. And if I feel like it, I might give you the number."

I stalked out and slammed the door behind me. Hard. I stopped at the hill, the concrete hill under the interstate. I had the same feeling, the feeling of being hardened. But this time there was more. The concrete was cold, too. Hard and cold. Maybe it was time, time for winter to last. Forever. Time for the cold to stay as well as the hard.

Mike's car slowly pulled up under the hill. He jumped the curb and parked on the sidewalk. I wanted to laugh but just stared. He climbed up the slope and sat next to me. He stayed quiet for a long time, almost like he was scared to say anything to me. And I didn't care to break the silence. I was just caught in a feeling, like one I'd had before, of being numb. Numb like death. Like I would pinch myself and not feel a thing. Numb all the way through. Numb fingers from the cold and numb mind from all year. Mike finally spoke, but if he hadn't, I wouldn't have cared. "It happened again, huh?"

"Yep."

He tried to smile at me but couldn't as his attempt faded into the cold air. "Your door slam threw me right off the couch."

"Sorry." Short. Curt.

"Why did you slam the door so hard?"

"I'm pissed."

He laughed, sort of. Looking at me cut the laugh short, right into a sigh. "Jodi, come on. Ease up just a little, would you? You're like a loaded cannon ready to explode and let the cannon ball fly right now."

I half shrugged. "You got it."

He squeezed my shoulder. "Ease up some. Just a little. At least tell me what happened that made you slam the door like that and wake me up."

So I told him what Wayne had asked. And how it had sounded—like some accusation. Like he was worried that I was running around town and telling everybody what he was doing to me. And how I hadn't really just told anybody. All the people who knew had told me. And there were probably more. Plenty more. God knows how many more there were—those who could see and see it well, probably well enough to make them sick, even though they didn't say anything. These were all the people who didn't know me. Personally, anyway. These were just the people who kept quiet, hidden in the wings. But they knew—from experience, the type of experience that creates intuition, creates the knack of just knowing.

And I was out of breath. My guts had spilled all over the concrete and down the hill. Hard and cold and solid. So solid, but not like me. I was breaking. Just then, I was cracking up, falling down some other hill in my head. And Mike was hugging me, rocking me back and forth a little, saying things softly that I couldn't really hear inside the chaos in my head. Then I heard him whisper, "Go ahead and cry."

So I did.

26

I sipped on the coffee. The heat slid down my throat, warming me up, but only in the literal sense. I could still sense the concrete hill, cold and hard and rough—all like it was a part of me. I was wondering where Pat was…running late, I guess. Unusual. And why now? Why did this have to be happening right now while I was cold and hard? Why now when I knew our exchange of words would at least warm me up some, just a little?

My fingers drummed on the cold, vinyl-covered stools. Otherwise, I sat still on the seat, solidifying again and filling in the cracks, the cracks from earlier on the hill when I was with Mike. So easy this had become—smoothing it, smoothing out the roughness, the cracks—just trying to make everything seem like it was all okay, like nothing was breaking down, not the hill and not me, either. Not me. That's it. Keep saying it's not real and it can't hurt.

A voice intruded. "Christ, sweetie, what're you thinking about this morning?"

I jumped and looked up at Pat. Again something had to break through an intense focus, an obsession, where I had the entire world tuned out enough to where I couldn't hear. And I wondered right then. I wondered if that had anything to do with the feeling of just being numb, where there is no feeling, or little at best. I smiled weakly. "Good morning, Pat."

She intently stared at me over the top of those reading glasses. Again. "So," she started in her Southern drawl enough to make me look back at her and pay attention because I had never heard a one syllable word dragged out this long before. "I suppose you've decided not to go hiding the evidence under the makeup. Not today, anyway."

"Yeah," I sighed. "Not today."

She gave me an affirmative nod. "Good."

I sipped the coffee, a little confused. "Good? Doesn't seem good to me."

Pat fixed her coffee. She wasn't humored at all, yet she was smiling. Sort of. A half smile, maybe. She scratched her head and watched her coffee as she stirred it. I wondered if she was looking for answers, like reading tea leaves. Finally, she sadly grinned at me. "Using makeup wasn't just lying to others—it was lying to yourself somehow."

"Really? Somehow? Then how?"

She shrugged, sipping her coffee. "It's not that complicated, Jodi. This has all been like a show and tell game. You've told me a lot. And I have relied on your word. That's okay, in a way. After all, I already knew." She stopped for a minute, staring off into space, then asking the waitress for an English muffin and strawberry jam. Then she turned back to me. "But what have I seen up until now—to show me the degree? Nothing, really. Most of my opinion has been a shot in the dark, but now with the naked eye I can see the degree of the abuse. Seeing isn't the same as hearing a story. Seeing adds a whole new dimension. I don't have to rely on my own sorry ass opinion or my wild imagination."

I hadn't thought about any of this, not at all. Pat said she had relied on my word, but hearing and seeing aren't the same. This still didn't explain what that had to do with me. "Well, Pat, what does not showing it to anyone else have to do with lying to myself?"

Her fingertips drummed absently on the counter. After a long moment of silence, she said, "Well, when you were just telling, even if everything you said was accurate, the depth was still covered. And not just to me and the rest of the world, but to your own self, too. When you looked in the mirror with your makeup on, you didn't see any more than I did. Hiding it from me? From others? From the public in general? Does any of that matter really? Most importantly, you were hiding it from yourself, too." She shrugged and smiled seriously. "Just another mild form of self-denial." Her eyebrows shot up as she continued. "But now? You aren't the only woman I've ever known standing where you are right now. And showing matters. What I've seen in the past, once this begins, is it is the first step in being honest with yourself and the beginning of pulling away. Maybe you feel like you need to be honest with others, like me, but it's far more important for you to keep being honest with yourself. This is the first move I've seen you take away from self-denial. And I think that's good."

Showing the world. Just not caring to cover up when I left. I had interpreted that as just meaning that I didn't care at all. I had thought all of that was negative, and here Pat was, letting me know there was something positive in the mix, like the flip side of a coin where I had been staring at one side so long that I didn't know the other side was there. Maybe the direction was changing, and maybe I could step beyond all this. Somehow, someday. Maybe I was moving towards the right path. Maybe it was positive. Maybe it was. I sure had thought differently. I had spent a long while now trapped in negative interpretations of what was going on. And that's what I had believed. "Thanks, Pat."

She patted my shoulder. "You're quite welcome."

Opposing thoughts can go with this game of show and tell, a game of the senses where the show and tell of the self creates the conflict, an inner conflict. Suddenly, no longer is anything certain about what to think or what to believe. Yet, this is all so simple, so easy. And so beliefs can change, then, just like the direction of the wind.

27

A nervous wreck, I shifted back and forth in the chair, uneasy. I started racking my brain, going through my memory file. What had I done? I must've done something. They had called me from work and asked me to come in a little early. And I was here early for whatever this was, a little early and waiting, waiting. The time asked to be there had passed, and this just made me more nervous. I chewed a little on what remnants of fingernails I had. I saw Ms. Woodhouse at the entrance door, and I let out a sigh of relief. Relief swept over me like a wave on the beach. At least I could get this over with. Ms. Woodhouse smiled at me. "Good afternoon, Jodi. Sorry I'm late."

I smiled back. "No problem. What's up?"

As she smiled again, my nervousness slipped away. "There was a discussion the other day on one of your days off. April has chosen to step down out of the head waitress position. An unplanned staff meeting was called. It was your day off and we couldn't get ahold of you. In your absence, you were nominated and then elected for the position. If you want the job, it's yours."

"Elected?" What a surprise.

She looked at me curiously. "Yeah. You didn't think this was anything bad, did you?"

I laughed. What a change. The knot in my stomach had disappeared. "I was trying to figure out what I had done."

Ms. Woodhouse laughed with me. "You've done everything right. That's all. So you want the job?"

I grinned, nodding. "Sure." More hours, a raise, more money, and less time with the beast. And less time in the horror flick fairy tale. What more could I ask for? This all sounded like Paradise. I'd be insane to pass up such an opportunity. Downright insane. And a promotion after three months on a job? What a boost that was. I spent the evening running around on a cloud. This was the best type of high— one based on being happy. I hadn't felt a rush like that in a real long time, so long that I had forgotten how such a moment felt. Hell, I had even forgotten that such a moment was possible. I savored the feeling, trusting that moments like this are out there, for anyone, including me.

28

As I rode the late night bus home, I stared out the window, wishing. When life seems to improve on one end, people tend to think that it will on the other. And I sat in the bus seat, just wishing. Dreaming some, but knowing—just knowing. I wasn't even quite near the stop where I would exit the bus, but the knack I had of just knowing was already setting in like always. And the knack was right. Wayne's loud snore that seemed to accompany his drinking greeted me when I opened the door, like always. I dozed off in my chair.

"Why are you sleeping over there?" startled me from my slumber.

Startled awake, I almost fell off the chair, grabbing the leather arm to keep from sliding off. The euphoric high from the previous night returned in thought but not in feeling. The rush was gone, stored only on the brain. And it wasn't even worth sharing at this point. Wishing and dreaming had all been overpowered by the knack—the knack of just knowing. I yawned. "Don't know. Must've sat down when I got home and just dozed off."

"You've done that a few times."

I shrugged. "So what?"

His eyes glared through me. "I want you in bed at night."

I stared at him as my chest tightened. I felt like I had an inner cat, a tiger, pacing—pacing back and forth, furious and looking for prey. Yet on the outside, this was smoothed over, just a fur ball of a kitten with an outer appearance of helplessness. As the inner tiger paced, I thought *it isn't going to stay this way—not anymore*. When I spoke, my voice came out flat and even. "Sorry about that," I said, although I knew I wasn't. "Thing is, I can't stand the smell of whiskey. I don't want it in my face when I'm trying to go to sleep. So why don't you just quit drinking?" Silence answered me, and suddenly I liked this, I liked it a lot—the helpless kitten feeling vindictive. About being angry, about cracking up on the hill and feeling cold and hard, and about the disgust for letting myself get pushed that far. "So," I continued, "Why don't I come to bed? Well, why don't you quit hurting me? We were together a long time before that started. And I just don't understand. Why do you keep going? Wayne, every time you hit me and every time you drink, you just push me further away. And you want me in bed with you at night? Next to you? Funny. I just don't feel I belong there anymore."

Silence lingered in the air and it felt really strange. As much as the silence was awkward and unwanted, a response sure wasn't wanted, either. So I just gazed up at the wooden ceiling, surrounded by the duality of uneasiness and relief. And I just sat there, swaying between calm and crazy, calm and crazy at the same time. I breathed the silence that I wanted to end while I hoped it never would, wishing it would solidify and turn to stone and vaporize all at the same time. But in reality, silence only works one way—it inevitably ends. And this happened when Wayne responded, "Why do you stay here, then?"

I leaned back in the chair and looked away, swallowed by the void of absence, of nowhere. Sometimes all anyone wants is a place. And that feeling of having nowhere to go was what I had been sensing, that was what I had been saying, and that's what I had convinced myself of, so that's what I had been believing, too. And believing is half of anything. Right then, though, I knew that place was just a minor problem. Hearing the question coming from

In the Air

Wayne put me much closer to admitting the truth, maybe because I was closer to the reality and closer to the problem. But I also wasn't far enough away right then, not far enough away to quit hearing in my head those same words: keep saying it's not real and it can't hurt. I finally said, "Hell, Wayne, I guess you quit loving me and let me go sometime back in February when you smacked me through the wall. Love is something I'm just not sure of anymore. Not on my part. But I know I haven't let you go."

He sighed. "I haven't let you go, either, Jodi."

I shrugged. "To me, you have. To me, you have to let a person go before you can push away, before you can shove someone around as hard as you've been shoving me."

He didn't respond to that. And I watched him. In that instant, sadness draped over his face. He rolled over in the bed and, with his back towards me, he let out another long sigh. I suppose truth hurts.

29

Thanksgiving had already arrived. This is traditionally the real beginning of the holidays, the season to be jolly—starting each year on Thanksgiving. And as it came, I could only find myself wondering, caught in relapse and wondering what the hell I had to be thankful for. And I sat on the stairs for a while, the outside stairs, in the cold November air, wondering. My mind came up empty, blank of reasons for thankfulness.

I had done this every year clear back to second grade. I made sure that, on every Thanksgiving, I would spend a few minutes alone, just to think and to thank. I routinely thought over the year, remembering the blessings just like I thought everybody should. And in these moments, I would give thanks for what I had, not for what I wanted. I did that at least once a year, and always on Thanksgiving. And I gave thanks for my happiness and wellbeing. So this was new to me. This had all become a new type of Thanksgiving.

In the Air

And I kept on and on, longer than normal, much longer, wondering what the hell I had to be thankful for because all I could think about was Wayne. All I could think about was abuse and alcohol and tense conversations and fights. Or exchanges, violent exchanges. Sometimes those violent exchanges were just words, but weapons nevertheless.

I remembered Wayne's question that had almost made me explode like a volcano, the one that had made me crack, the one that had made me break down just a couple weeks earlier on the hill—the concrete hill that was cold and hard and rough. That had been on the day the cold front had come through and the heavy air had hit me in the face. And I had liked the cold air. I remembered it. And I remembered the whole day, all in a few seconds, just in a flash.

And I smiled. I could feel the joy in the smile creeping up on me. I could feel it on the outside and on the inside. Yeah, this life was tough, all right. The whole year had been a disaster, and it was rough, but I had not toughed it out on my own. I had not been alone. This was all in that question Wayne had asked me about who I told. No one. Instead, this was who told me. Those who knew already—Mike, Pat, April. They were different people who knew for different reasons who had all spoken out and spoken for the same reason.

Because they cared—about me. My three guardian angels. What more could I be thankful for? Right now? On this Thanksgiving? My three guardian angels. Priceless. Damn, I must be lucky. Real lucky.

30

I was not in the mood to go sit under the hill. But I needed to get away for a while. The walks had become few and far between. But I needed them. Badly. I only seemed to be able to go through this ritual on my days off, and now, as the head waitress at work, I only had two instead of three. I really had thought working more would be better for me. That would be less time at home with the beast. But this also meant less time for my ritual, less time to take this walk, which had come to mean a lot to me. The walk had become an important factor for me, just to survive and keep myself balanced off the edge of tumbling over the line of insanity. Ah hell. Guess I had stayed close, close enough, anyway.

And the air was colder now. That was how I liked it—cold enough to walk briskly and stay comfortable at the same time if I wanted to. I liked having choice. I liked the option because it made me feel like I had control of myself. Control—of my time. Control—of my mood because I could expend the aggression inside of me. Just control. Somehow that mattered.

"Mind if I come along?"

I grinned as Mike joined me in stride, a little short on breath. He must have been running to catch up with me as I had already made it halfway to the turn in the road. "Of course not."

"Damn, Jodi, you're never home anymore. I've had a few times that I've been out here walking all by my lonesome."

I laughed. "Ah, bullshit."

He shook his head. "I'm serious. You're the one who got me into this habit, and now I do it more than you do." I could tell he was talking in a humorous tone while he wasn't really joking around. "So why don't we go at night sometime, when you get off of work?" he suggested.

I stopped. "Mike, it's turning into winter for Christ's sake. It's been getting down into the twenties at night sometimes."

He stuck out his lower lip, pretending to pout. "Wimp."

The humor beneath the serious act made me laugh again. "Okay. Maybe. But why? Why are you being so insistent right now about this?"

He fell quiet until we reached our usual stop and plopped down into the grass. He sighed. "I don't know. I feel like I'm slipping, like I'm not staying on top of the situation. Almost like something might happen just because I'm not paying attention. I keep telling you. I've seen all this before. Not keeping in touch with you better is just bugging me."

I looked sideways at him. "Go to hell, Mike. You usually know more than I do about my life with Wayne. What's the real reason?"

He grinned, like a kid caught with his hand in the cookie jar. "I've been teaching you too much. Okay. Being bugged is part of it, but I've been missing the walks, too. I didn't realize how much I enjoyed them until they dwindled down to about once a week, twice if I'm lucky."

I laid back in the grass. "So what do you do when you go on walks alone?"

"Think."

"Think about what?"

He sighed. "About what a fool I am."

"For what?"

He rolled over on his side, and his dark eyes looked straight at me. "For falling in love with you." The wave of surprise washed over me, making me feel strangely warm on the near frozen ground beneath me. He continued, "Yep. For falling in love with you when I know we can never take that anywhere—except around this long block." He kissed my forehead. "On long walks."

I smiled. As dangerous as such a truth could be, my spirit lifted. To feel love and know it was close was a great thing to feel, even if it couldn't go any further than it already was, even if could never really be had in whole. I stared off into the black sky, accepting this for what it was. Angels can't be had, anyway.

31

I sat on the concrete hill, feeling troubled. As good or bad as anything felt, depending on what I thought about, just the fact that both sides were there wasn't right. Good points. Bad points. There aren't supposed to be any good points about nightmares.

Allowing abuse to the self. That's a nightmare, isn't it? What else could that be? Just a major inconvenience while seeking out something else? What a road to travel, especially when the goal isn't reachable. Good and bad. That's how it goes in fairy tales. Fairy tales aren't supposed to be true at all, yet all of this was happening to me—too real—and getting scarier by the day.

Pulling away. I gazed at the whizzing cars and, as they travelled off into the distance, I realized I was pulling away from Wayne and becoming attached to Mike at the same time. And Mike—admitting how he felt when we were on the walk. Wayne—the representation of jealousy. Hell, the dangerous type, too, that would kill just for that reason alone—the jealousy. Mike was crazy for loving me, just crazy. And I had no room to talk, either.

Ambivalence. I was just used to being hit at this point. Alcohol. That was something I had already been used to all my life. I pictured my grandmother throwing that large glass ashtray across the living room at my grandfather, then remembered the time when my mom weaved the lanes of Interstate 10 in Los Angeles at 90 miles an hour while I sat in the passenger seat, praying to see the next day. Abuse and alcohol were what I tolerated together while each was bad enough alone. Together they were dangerous—deadly. No doubt about it. And for what?

All I did was seek ideals and look for what I thought was perfect. I seemed to set goals that were out of reach, looking for a hero or an angel I could have, alive on earth. Crazy. This way of thinking was just crazy. I had to be out of my head. I had to be.

I stayed on the hill for a long time, at least two hours, stuck to the concrete, just feeling troubled. Just wondering what my head had been telling me, trying to see what I had been thinking deep down in the subconscious. Had I been believing? Had I been thinking that I could step past Wayne and have Mike? When had this sick notion developed? When did it really start?

No, it wasn't just the night before, on the walk. This had to have been there for a while. For a long while. I should have been long gone a long time ago. Somewhere deep in my subconscious was a crazy idea that I could have a relationship with Mike. Maybe I could just push Wayne aside and walk away with Mike. Somewhere in the mess in my head, I had been thinking that, and believing it, too, for longer than I knew.

Believing that—scary. I sat on the hill, entranced by the sound of the cars as they whizzed by over top of me. These thoughts were scary to think at all, let alone believe in, just like this was all some fairy tale and somehow I was going to make it out alive and live happily ever after. How terrifying—to trust the end of fairy tales—and to believe in them—when the story was the chaos I lived in, very real, and right off the edge of insanity.

32

I was caught, trapped in the V of Wayne's elbow. And thoughts became busy in my head, too busy again, trying to figure out what the hell I could have said. And too busy again, trying to create a new category for this. Up on the throat instead of down. Pull instead of push. Yeah, this was a whole new method. Damn. Thought I had figured it all out. Thought I didn't have anything left to learn and at least knew what was coming. Maybe I should've listened—to Wayne, actually. As I stood there half choked, I could visualize the needles falling out of the ceiling, just like magic. And he had told me, he had forewarned me then the day he had said, "When you think you know it all, baby, you realize you don't." And this hold he had me in was new, all right.

And I was caught, ensnared in the V of his arm, and too busy, too busy speculating on how this was new. Again. Too busy to realize that I was being strangled. And again,

In the Air

this was for nothing, nothing worth remembering, too trivial to merit such a consequence. I just couldn't understand. Why had he blown? What had I said that made him blow into a rage enough to stand behind me and hold me this way while choking and shaking me as physical exclamation points behind his profanities.

Choke. I began to feel dizzy while my nails dug, clawing, but they weren't doing anything. Wayne was yelling something, but I couldn't hear what he was saying. I tried to because maybe he was telling me. Maybe he was identifying what I had said to spark his temper. Just maybe. But I couldn't hear anything. His voice seemed to be off in the distance, just too far away for me to understand him.

So was this it? Was this what Mike had really meant when he had said that Wayne would push my head back under the water? Drowning. I was drowning without the water. Being strangled—same difference. Was this it? Was this really it? Specks. Little specks. My eyes were open, but all I could see were a million little specks against something else—they bounced continuously off some hole. Out of it. And I could vaguely see the darkness beyond the specks. Black. Very, very black. This must have been death.

33

When I came to, I was hugging the bottom rail of the outside staircase. I had no idea of how long I had been there—could have been hours, even a day or two. I might have believed that if someone had told me that I had just been sitting there in some catatonic state. Mike was next to me, silent, trying to unwind my grip from the pole. I asked, "How long have you been here, Mike?" and my voice came out strange, sounding loud in my inner ear yet distant at the same time.

His grim look stayed on my fingers as he peeled them one by one from the pole. "That doesn't matter. So how long have you been out here nearly glued to this staircase?" His voice sounded closer to normal, but I could tell it was just a whisper.

"I don't know."

"What happened?"

I could only think of specks. "I don't know."

"Come on, Jodi. Tell me."

In the Air

I kept trying to remember and kept seeing specks. "I don't remember right now. I really don't."

"Think then." He sighed, watching my fingers recling the pole. He quit trying to loosen me out of my pole hug for a while. He moved up a step and started rubbing my shoulders slowly and firmly. "Damn, kid, you're as hard as a rock."

He kept rubbing along the top of my shoulders and this kept feeling good until fear gripped me suddenly when his hands reached the back of my neck. A chill swept through me as the fear escalated into terror, and instantly I was filled full of dread and panic without knowing why. Not knowing where this came from created another dimension— fear just of fear. And then it came—the memory came, crashing back along some tidal brain wave. Specks. The black hole. The V that I had been caught in. They all came back at once. I looked at Mike. "I thought I was dead."

"So what happened?" he asked softly.

And I told him about the specks, the black hole, the V I was caught in, unable to move. And how I had wondered if I was drowning and wondered how that could be while I was standing in the air. And I told him how I had really thought I was seeing death. How I had tried to listen to what Wayne was saying but couldn't hear a thing. How I had tried to breathe but couldn't. All I could do was stare at a million little specks bouncing off of some black hole somewhere, the hole I was convinced was death. And I was sure, damn sure, that I was going to be heading down that hole the last I remembered.

With a long sigh, Mike stayed silent and held me, and I had the same feeling again, just like that time up on the concrete hill when I was cracking, cracking up. But Mike was different this time because, as he held and rocked me like a baby, I could feel him tremble, too. Just a little, just a touch, but enough to be noticed. I wasn't alone any longer, not in the inner chill. He kept wiping my tears away until they slowed down. "Hey," he said softly, "Let's take a walk. I think we could both use one."

We didn't move fast or at our normal pace. We moved much slower than usual, trudging down the sidewalk. I had been too scared to check on Wayne upstairs, so Mike had. Wayne was passed out on a fifth of Jack Daniels. So it was okay to move slowly. I was boiling hot, ready to let the snow blow off the top of my volcano. Asleep. Whiskey. And that's while I had been outside, glued to the pole and comatose. I talked about it calmly. And my voice was quiet, strangely quiet and level, enough to spook me. I couldn't understand the mindset. I couldn't understand how a person could almost kill somebody, then get drunk and go to sleep. No heart. That's just no damn heart. I swallowed hard. "This is just getting worse."

Mike stopped me on the sidewalk. "Did you hear yourself? Did you hear what you just said out loud?"

"What?"

He grinned. "That it's getting worse. I told you months ago, months, that this was all just getting started. It would get worse. I've been calling it all since day one." His smile faded. "But now it hurts me to see you getting hurt."

"What's the point?"

"Get out of here, Jodi. I can't believe you're still here. Just get out." He sighed again and looked away. We walked for a while, up towards the bend, and just stayed quiet. We reached the resting spot and sat down on the grass even though neither of us was tired. This was just a habit for us. A habit and a good excuse not to be home. Following the routine, the ritual, we managed to receive a moment of stability and an escape from the madness. "If you stay after this, it'll probably end up getting nastier than I originally thought it would when I first told you to leave."

"Why?"

He shrugged, half-smiling, or trying to. But his smile disappeared as quickly as it had arrived. "That's easy. I didn't love you then."

Mike started rubbing my back again, my shoulders, and he worked slowly, slowly up to the neck. Building, building up, building trust—just like the one time we had made love, to remind me that somebody cared since all I was going to get anymore from Wayne was fucked. Suddenly, I got it. I understood what Mike had meant then. This wasn't just sex and romance. He had meant fucked over, maybe fucked up. Completely. And Mike was rubbing my neck, just reminding me again that just because one person strangles me doesn't mean that everybody will.

34

Almost Christmas, a week away. And the lack of anticipation all seemed a little strange. I wanted to be looking forward to it, but a few things just weren't there. I just didn't have it. Instead, I found myself pretending, going through the motions, just acting. That's what it felt like, some play I was in that I hadn't tried out for, and I was just a character on the stage playing a part and pretending to be what I wasn't. I could only pretend anticipation. And I tried very hard to pretend that I was looking forward to Christmas when I knew I didn't care—at all.

I remembered when I was five years old. My brother, who had an older friend with an older brother, spilled the beans to me. There was no such thing as a Santa Claus. I had gotten really upset and bawled my eyes out of tears. For days. When the truth was verified by all the family I asked, including Mom, I cried all the way through the first week of the next year.

But there still had been anticipation. If there had never been a Santa Claus, at least there would still be a bunch of presents.

But now it was gone. Anticipation was a word I could still use, still define, and still create sentences to show how it should be used. But it had become a feeling I couldn't feel, even though I actually tried to. And it all seemed strange, real strange, like all I could attach Christmas and anticipation to was the concrete hill under the interstate. Cold and hard, with the cars whizzing by overhead, whizzing off with hope. Just coming and going, coming and going. I suppose anticipation gets lost when enshrouded by cold and hard. Sort of like hope does, just whizzing by but not stopping in. And I tried to pretend. I really did. I tried to pretend that anticipation was there when I knew that I didn't care—at all.

35

When Christmas came, I had to work because Shoney's was open. I came home to a neighborhood party winding down. Almost everybody was trashed and ready to crash. Mike, though, was sober. Wayne was already upstairs and asleep. I asked Mike quietly, "So who are you? The designated driver to give everybody else a ride home, or what?"

He grinned. "No. I'm the designated proof for you to show that you are not the only sober soul left within a five hundred mile radius of the house."

I hugged him. "Thanks a lot."

Half an hour later, Mike had everybody out of the house. I was in the mood for a walk even though it was cold outside. Just a few houses away, Mike stopped me and held me in a tight hug for just a minute. "Hey. Merry Christmas."

"Yeah. Merry Christmas." I sighed as we resumed the walk. "I got a phone call today from my family."

He looked curiously at me. "You say that kind of strange, like it's out of the ordinary for you to get a call on Christmas. What's up?"

"Nothing, really. They just called to wish me a Merry Christmas." I reflected on the moment—just that feeling. That knack for knowing and the sick way it made me feel. They weren't drunk when they called, not during the call, but I could tell from places and people mentioned that they would be before the night was out. "Mike, have I ever told you about my family? Alcoholism is almost a given."

He shook his head and shrugged at the same time. "I don't think we've ever talked about it, but I sort of figured that to be a part of your past anyway. When you and Wayne were first together, he told me that you said if he wanted you to be his girlfriend, then he had to give up the alcohol. People would only create a condition like that if they already know how much it can hurt. So, what's up? Did you tell them what's going on?"

I leaned back against an oak tree trunk. "No. I just told them everything is fine. That's all they know. And that's part of the problem—what we've talked about before about me leaving."

In the Air

"What does your family have to do with you not getting out of here?"

I looked into the black sky. "Because the thought of going there makes me wonder what's the lesser of the two evils. Here or the place that got me here to begin with."

"Did you get slapped around as a kid or something?"

I stretched out in the grass, closing my eyes, remembering. "No. But tell me what's worse, that or the alcohol. My family is full of alcoholics. What hurts the most—the body, the mind, or the soul? Doesn't seem to matter where I go—something hurts. So what's the worst?"

Mike squeezed my hand. "Hell, I don't know. Good questions. But I sure don't have any answers."

"Me, either." Stars started to shine in the black sky, uncovered from passing clouds. "I don't have any answers, either. And I suppose that's why I just don't feel like I have a place to go right now if I leave Wayne."

"Start looking here," Mike said. I glanced at him. Two fingers were resting on his chest and then on mine. "Start looking right here for a place. On the inside of yourself."

36

The New Year came in, and with it came a relief. For me, anyway. Just making it through the holidays had been tough, real tough—all the symbolism about love and God and Jesus and giving and forgiving. All of this had messed with my head and kept my thoughts on a constant spin, spinning furiously and leaving me feeling like the times I had spun and fallen out on the grass. I had been feeling strangely like that for a while without the action. And now with the New Year in, I wasn't feeling quite so dizzy.

I made it to the coffee shop. The air was freezing outside. Pat was already warmed up inside with her cup of coffee. "Hey, Pat. Happy New Year."

"No kidding, sweetie. The holidays are now officially over. You had me worried there for a while. You look better today than you have for weeks. So, tell me. What's your new year's resolution?"

In the Air

I shrugged, stirring my coffee. "Nothing."

"Well, listen…" She hesitated, sipping her coffee. "If you decide to get around to making a resolution such as to not put up with the shit that you've been putting up with, just let me know." She patted her pocketbook. "I've saved up enough spare change to buy you a plane ticket out of here. Just let me know when you're ready to go."

I looked at her, surprised. "When did you save money for a plane ticket?"

She smiled as her eyebrows shot up a second. "A little here. A little there. For the last six months. Just a little so I wouldn't really miss it. And now I think there's plenty to cover an airplane ticket as long as it stays in the continental U.S. So when you reach the point of being ready, let me know."

I sipped on my coffee, feeling strangely warm, strangely safe, knowing suddenly that there was a touch of sanity right outside that feeling of dizziness. A feeling of balance, coming from someone who cared. Knowing such a thing was there! A strong sense of relief swept through me as I realized how much Pat truly cared. This was better than the relief I had already felt about the holidays being over. "Thanks, Pat."

She smiled. "You're welcome, sweetie."

Jodi Sullivan

"I'll try to come up with that resolution."

"Sounds good. Better yet, just do it."

37

Wayne blocked me at the doorway. With each of his hands on the door frame, I couldn't walk by him. I waited for him to get out of the way, but he just stared at me. I sighed. "Why are you doing this?"

He tilted his head back. "I'd like to talk to you."

I stood still for a few seconds, wondering if I should just say no or act indifferent. His arms in front of me while blocking my exit from the door made me feel strange. Electrified, trapped. I sighed. "Talk about what?"

"Us."

I stared at him. What a waste, what a fucking waste. If he only had a heart. I took a long look at his face. Usually so handsome, but his brown eyes had become sunk in his head. Deep. "What about us?"

"We haven't made love since the beginning of December. That's more than a month."

I kept staring at him. He had to be immune. He had to be. Immune to the pain I felt. Perhaps just completely immune to the reality of what he had done to me. Either that or his memory just sucked. The last thing I could be feeling was any sexual attraction. "Wayne, you're crazy."

"No, I'm not. It's been a month."

I shivered, taken by a sudden wonder of what it would feel like when I stepped outside. And I realized I was right. He was crazy—totally out of his head. He stood there talking to me as if he had absolutely no recollection of holding me in the V, practically choking me to death, so I figured I might as well give him a recap. "Wayne, the last time we argued, you almost killed me. And you want me to make love to you?"

He looked down his nose at me with disdain, then rolled his eyes. "What are you talking about? I didn't hurt you at all."

A laugh of utter disbelief escaped me. I couldn't believe what I was hearing. But the tone of his voice—that's what I was really hearing. There was no doubt in his voice at all—not an inkling. To him, what he was saying was just a factual statement. A tightness crept across my chest. I could just tell—really know what he meant. He was making a statement, just a statement of what was, to him, a fact. And he was believing what he said. Meanwhile, all I could think in return was a vivid image of the specks, the million little specks I had seen, and the black hole that I had thought was death. Although I just wanted to scream, my voice came out so level and clear that I wondered who was talking. "Wayne, you hurt me that time. Real bad—the worst yet. Maybe you can't remember it, but I sure can. And if you don't believe what I'm saying, ask Mike. He's the one who found me outside. I wasn't in the best shape."

He drew away from the door. "Fine. I'll do just that. I'll ask Mike about it. And you better be right."

"Better be? Fuck you. I already know I am." I stalked out the door and into the cold air. I had that strange feeling again, like all of this was surreal. Weird, just a living nightmare. As I walked up Little Creek Road, one of the bank thermometers flashed twenty-two degrees. The walk felt warmer than my encounter with Wayne. This had to be a dream. It had to be.

38

I was really tired, exhausted from work. Sunday nights to me were like Fridays for others. I had the next two days off. This was a relief, a blessing in disguise, because I was really tired from five straight days of work. Two days off sounded like Paradise, or at least a welcome reprieve. I needed to rest.

Approaching the house, loud voices travelled in the air to my ears. I stood on the outside balcony staircase and listened. Mike and Wayne were arguing. Shit. There had been another time I had witnessed them while they argued. This happened shortly after I had arrived there. I could still picture the moment. Wayne had beat the shit out of Mike. Even though they were brothers, they were so different in size. Wayne was six inches taller and over thirty pounds heavier, enough to make me wonder about how they could be brothers.

In the Air

I moved slowly up the steps. I took one and stopped, then took two and waited awhile, like I didn't really want to be there but I didn't want to miss the show, either. I strained to listen through the closed oak door. And I kept moving closer until I could finally hear what they were saying, hear it loud and clear.

Yeah, they were arguing all right—about me. And I felt chilled. Tense, angry, frustrated voices slung words as if they were rocks. And Mike asked Wayne, "Why do you have to keep hurting Jodi? Why can't you just get ahold of yourself and quit drinking? Maybe get a job?"

Wayne answered, not the question but the tone. He answered the attitude, matching the feeling—anger. He yelled at Mike, "Why don't you just stay out of this and mind your own fucking business?"

Then there was noise, just noise. A thump against the wall echoed outside, and in my head, I visualized Wayne pushing Mike up against it. On impulse, I started to walk in because I wanted to break it up, but I stalled at the doorknob, reminding myself that I am not God. In my hesitation, I accepted that staying outside was a better option because it would probably be better for Mike if Wayne didn't know I was standing outside the door. I didn't need to start him wondering how long I had been there or what I had heard.

Outside seemed to be the best choice. So I sat down in a lawn chair on the patio and waited, listening to muffled profanities and fists pounding on flesh.

The fight stopped quicker than I expected. The outside air was freezing cold. I sat on a step so icy it made my buttocks go numb. I stared into the starlight, wondering how long I should wait before going inside. I stayed on the stairs, cold. I was tired, so tired, that I just wanted rest, wanted sleep. Then suddenly I found myself dreading that I had two days off and wishing that I was working the next day. A day's rest on the job? That just didn't sound right—must've been because I was just tired, so tired—exhausted all the way.

39

Then a seizure came. In the middle of an argument, it came. While every nerve already in me was electrified, it came. While I was letting the volcano erupt from within me, it came, crawling out from the pit of my stomach. As the seizure crept upward to my head, the argument suddenly ended, and the electrical charge from the anger blacked out. The volcano inside of me that had been ready to erupt remained right under the snow covered mountain because I wasn't there anymore.

While one side of my brain was disconnected from the other, I stared at a fuzz of itty bitty gold specks and watched sets of mixed red and blue dashes, what I always saw during a seizure, skirt across my range of vision. I wondered what I was doing. I always did some pretty weird things during a seizure, whether walk in circles, stiffen, or start masturbating—all while I wasn't even there. And I wondered if Wayne had noticed yet. The seizure would take about a minute, a minute and a half at the most, to finish. And I was disappointed already, even though still in an altered state. I had thought they were gone for good this time around. Since the grand mal seizure, two and a half years had passed. I had really believed they were under control and gone. For good. The seizure subsided. I returned to reality, greeted by a strong wave of disappointment, and found Wayne quiet and kneeling in front of me, scared and worried. "Are you okay?"

I almost laughed, but I swallowed this before it came out. Concern, real concern, covered his face and controlled his voice. His hands squeezed mine gently as a gesture of consolation. Kill me one day and love me the next. I sighed. "Welcome aboard. You have just witnessed a partial-complex seizure, Wayne."

"What should I do?"

I laughed. "Nothing. It's over. While it's happening, you can't really do much, either. It just comes and goes." Comes and goes like overhead traffic, whizzing by like hope. Gone again—hope now gone again for something else.

He was pale. "I thought you were dying." His face had lost color to where he looked like a ghost, something in him I had never seen—like a scared, little kid kneeling right in front of me, petrified. What a change. And I wished for a while, just a second or two, that the seizures were a controllable entity that I could use to stop arguments, use to avoid being hit, and use just to make him look like a frightened little child, just like he did right then.

I rejected the thought, pushed it away. What a crazy thought—insane. Seizures are dangerous, somewhat. And tiring, very tiring. "No, I wasn't dying. I just left the planet for a minute or so." I sighed. "Get used to what you saw. I guess my medicine has quit working. They'll probably keep coming now."

I stared off at nothing, wondering if I should call the doctor, whom I hadn't seen since I went ballistic on him because of the stupidity of his assessment that I was on cocaine and stormed out of the office two years earlier. And I wasn't sure if I could. I no longer had any health insurance and had no money to pay for an office visit. Oh well. And I was tired, real tired. And the seizures were back. Damn, damn, damn.

Exhausted, I don't remember hitting the pillow.

40

As I came around the waitress station to fill up some drinks, April and Debbie trapped me in a corner. Debbie piped, "Hey, you're spacey today."

I laughed. The two amazons had me pinned, waiting for an answer. Weather talk was history. Debbie didn't use it much anymore—just straight and to the point. "Yeah, I guess so."

"More alcohol?" Debbie asked flatly.

"No—not at all." My voice drifted off while my mind was still stuck on the seizure. "Listen," I suggested, "How about a bite after work?"

April grinned. "It's about time you got around to being the one to make suggestions."

The amazons zoomed off as quickly as they had come. I stood there in a daze. The first time they had talked me into going out for a bite was four months earlier. Since then, we had gone out many times. Was this the first time that going out was my idea? Hell, no. I couldn't be that oblivious to being sociable. But I thought hard, only to find that I couldn't ever remember initiating the idea. Damn, I was lost, so out of touch that I had become socially inept. I really hated the thought that I was that far gone.

We slid into the diner's booth. After the server brought us drinks and took our order, Debbie laid out the cards fast. And all I could think was how she ought to be a card dealer in Vegas. "Okay," she said, "What's up?"

Debbie and April already knew about the seizures. That had just been a part of past conversations over eggs and hamburgers in the middle of the night. I sighed. The topic was easy to talk about before while I was believing the seizures were gone. But now they were back, holding me, just like Wayne, just like the V. So it wasn't so easy now to talk about the seizures. I swallowed hard. "It's the epilepsy, y'all. The seizures I've told you about that I used to have all the time. They're back."

For a short while, they just sat and stared at me, paralyzed, looking as if they were frozen in time, just like a picture looks on the television screen when the motion suddenly stops. I wanted to laugh, but it wasn't funny. I figured they were reacting like others I had known had in the past—they just didn't know what to say. Debbie finally broke the silence. "Well, what can we do for you?"

I shrugged. "Nothing." The waitress delivered our food, and the conversation fell silent—the type of silence that's heavy. Even the waitress looked nervous. Inside of me, I could feel the fear and paralysis reemerging—again. And I could feel me struggling, trying to push all of this away and trying to control the fear so it wouldn't control me. And the silence made the fear stronger, much stronger because there wasn't anything there to distract it. Finally, the food was down and the waitress was gone. I sighed, relieved. "The problem is, you can't do anything. But if you see me out wandering around on the floor and doing anything weird, please pull me off and take me back to the waitress station, okay?"

"Sure," April said as she bit into her hamburger. "That's what friends are for."

41

April dropped me off past two a.m. I had to cheer them up somehow. So I told stories about some crazy moments that had happened other times during past seizures. Sometimes the memory could be funny because I really had done some wild acts, like standing up abruptly and walking out of class or quitting my talking in mid-sentence. And part of being able to live with seizures was learning how to laugh at them once in a while. Sometimes these were like having Halloween year round as much as I would scare the hell out of everyone around me. Often during a seizure, people would think I was dying because of the choking noise I often made. Then the seizure would end, and I would tell them I was fine, and they would laugh, sometimes laugh hard while telling me what strange act I had done that time. And they would laugh some more, just the comical relief that follows fear—just like Halloween.

Mike was waiting at the foot of the staircase when I got home. His drawn face looked somewhere between tired and pissed. "Damn, you're late. I've been sitting here waiting for you since midnight."

I shrugged. "Didn't know I had a curfew."

My words bit him and his eyes narrowed. Silence fell between us. Fear rushed in just like the night I had rushed to the woods and Mike had promised that he wouldn't quit caring.

Again, my heart slid out my sleeve, ready to be crushed as it sat in the open on a wire ready to snap from the tension. Again, I felt the release. Deep...I breathed real deep. Mike's voice was soft. "True. Let's go for a walk."

I quickly changed clothes and skipped a shower until later. I could tell Mike was real aggravated so, as soon as we started walking, I opened up the conversation because I couldn't stand the silence. The air was just too heavy. "What's up?"

"A few things." He kept his gaze on the sidewalk while he thought, then looked straight at me. "Do you talk to Wayne like that?"

"Like what?"

He thumbed the house behind us. "Like you did to me back there. You were pretty sarcastic, talking like a bitch. I waited two hours because I was concerned, and your response was you don't have a curfew."

I stopped and thought for a while, aware that I had wondered countless times what had started the arguments with Wayne. And I really hadn't known. Sarcasm was something that came so natural to me that, while in school, I constantly got reprimanded for words that had escaped my mouth prior to thinking about what they meant. But I had never paid any high price for what I said. After time, I suppose being this way just seemed comfortable and familiar while not knowing how much familiarity breeds contempt. "I don't know," I said to Mike's question. "I really don't know if I talk like that to Wayne. I guess I might have."

"You really ought to think about that, Jodi. I had a strong surge of anger right then that took me a minute to control. If you had been a guy, I probably would have cold cocked you." I pulled away, but Mike gently pulled me back. "Calm down. I didn't do any such thing. I just want you to know the urge was there and why it was."

Suddenly, I didn't care about the silence. As bad as it felt, there was something good about it. And we walked. Mike slowed me down three times with gentle tugs. No words were spoken. Inside, I could feel a volcano hissing. I was edgy. Nervous. And finally, I couldn't handle the silence. "Okay, what else is going on? You were worried and waiting for a reason, and we haven't gotten to that yet.

Jodi Sullivan

How come I just know something really screwed up is going on and I just don't know what it is yet?"

Mike went straight to the point. "Wayne drank a full fifth of Jack Daniels tonight."

"Top to bottom, huh?"

"Yeah."

I sighed. "So what? Kind of like a junkie, I guess. When the high doesn't come easy anymore, just increase the dosage."

Mike pulled me down in the grass. "Relax," he said. "Well, he was muttering something about you having a seizure yesterday while you guys were right in the middle of an argument."

I shrugged, remembering Wayne's frightened look and gentle touch when I had come out of the seizure. "Yeah, I had one. That's what happened."

"Drunk, he just kept muttering that he didn't know if it was real or not. If you were faking it, he said, he was going to beat the living shit out of you." Mike glanced at me. I could tell he didn't want to say what he was thinking. He sighed. Nervous, just like I had been with April and Debbie. It's easy to talk about a topic that feels like it has no grip, like it's all just a part of the past. But when the grip changes, and the truth or meaning cannot be certain, talking about it can be hard. "Listen," Mike finally asked, "It was real, wasn't it?"

Indignant, I tossed my head. "Yes. I already told you I had one. It was real, all right, and pretty scary after going so long without one."

We laid in the grass for a while. Mike had worried about whether or not the seizure was real. And I could tell he felt better now just knowing that it had actually occurred because of what Wayne had said. Somehow, that felt kind of sickening because the fact that it was real was already devastating in itself, to me. Yet the reality was also a relief. Strange.

Before we reached the house, Mike stopped me on the sidewalk and gave me a hug, and it was a gesture I really needed right then. He half laughed. "I feel better now, knowing it was a real one. That doesn't sound right. I'm sorry it happened. Really."

I tried to smile as the tears welled up. "Thanks."

Mike hugged me again just to remind me one more time. Just once. Remind me that not everyone says things that hurt. Fake seizures! How can I fake what I can't see and can't control? Mike tousled my hair. "You're welcome."

42

I sat on the hill, cold and hard, looking at the snow—four inches of it from the night before. The whiteness covered everything, anything that it could reach from the rooftops to the top limbs of the highest oaks. But it couldn't reach where I was, under the interstate. And I just sat there on the hard, frozen concrete, thinking. Dark gray clouds blanketed the sky. They looked ready to fall out again and add another layer of white, hide something else some more, as if four inches just wasn't enough.

Wasn't enough. February 4th was only three days away and, like the four inches of snow, last year's experiences on February 4th hadn't been enough, either.

Christ, this had been going on for a whole year. Like a fool, I had stayed, thinking this was loyalty. But all I had stayed for was more of the same, like the first time wasn't enough. And now the weirdness—the strange way that numbers seemed to recur and the oddity of first times. Oh, how the first time just keeps coming back, stronger than any of the other times, just because it was the beginning.

And I tried to remember other factors, like the number of times that Mike had just flat out said to me, "Get out of here." I don't know how many times I had heard him say that to me. Lost count. And I really couldn't remember how many arguments there had been between Wayne and me. Hell. I had stuffed away trying to keep a count on that back in the summer. Numbers just didn't seem important then. And I couldn't tally the number of conversations that I had had with Pat or April and Debbie. These all blended together like they had been thrown together in some wild soup recipe and pureed.

But I didn't forget the first time, and the strength of how I had felt then was back, the sense of suddenly not feeling safe anymore. That first time, I had stood there, stripped of any protector. Suddenly I laid next to some monster from a fairy tale that I didn't even know. I slept with a man who had become a stranger to me and still was one. I stared at the concrete. Almost a year. A whole fucking year! With this much time, I had done nothing, nothing but tolerate the abuse and let it just get worse. I had been that deer, frozen in position, while staring into the headlights and hearing the blaring horn of the oncoming eighteen wheeler.

I chewed my lower lip. Mike had warned me from the onset that everything would just get worse, and I hadn't listened. I didn't heed his warning when he had said to me, "Wayne's been your lover for two years. He's been my older brother all my life." I hadn't listened because I didn't want to believe that this was true. I just didn't want to. And believing is half of anything. And believing was half the reason I was sitting here on the hill, under the interstate, while the traffic whizzed by above me, like hope. Coming and going, coming and going.

A year. A whole damn year. I stared out across what I could see from underneath the interstate. White, solid white, so bright that my eyes hurt. White like the dress that a bride wears. So beautiful, so quiet, so white, and therefore so pure and so innocent. And it was almost to the day. One year, just like an anniversary, almost to the day. And I stayed underneath the interstate, looking at the cracks, up and down and through the concrete, just like the cracks that were running through me. And when I thought about me and what was inside, I could only see an empty, dark void. I did not see the whiteness of the snow that was so white, and pure and not yet disturbed.

43

Up at the drugstore coffee bar, Pat and I had sat drinking coffee for about an hour. I had finished my fourth cup, so I pulled out the money for the coffee and the tip and laid it on the counter. I was ready to go. "Listen, Jodi," Pat said as she patted my arm, "I saw my doctor yesterday and I asked him a few questions."

I turned to look at her. "About what?"

"About seizures and what causes them. We got into a pretty long talk. He ended up telling me that stress plays a pretty big role in the life of someone who has seizures." One of her eyebrows shot up as she sat back to take a good look at me. Then she continued, "And what you've been going through sure causes a lot of stress."

I sat back down and had my coffee filled back up. "Pat, it's not that easy."

"Hopefully, my doctor knows more about this than you or I do."

I shrugged. "Maybe he does. Maybe he doesn't. After all, I have the damn things. I hope I know more than he does. Stress can play some role, but there are other factors that are just as important, or even more important. Like noise and lights and sleep. Or it could be like what happened before, where my body just rejected the medicine."

"Could be," Pat parroted. "Yeah, just like the stress might have been the reason. Listen, don't downplay the possibility so much. You piss me off when you do that, and you're doing it right now."

I stayed quiet. Yeah, I guess I was downplaying, a real sign of denial. Just downplay what happens like it isn't important, like it just doesn't matter, like it doesn't contribute at all to my physical health and it just isn't a factor. Downplaying—just a way to deny the reality of something that exists. How many times had I downplayed in the last year? How many truths or simple facts had I denied? Or ignored? Or conveniently sidestepped while knowing they were important factors at the same time? I did that. I did it a lot. And it didn't matter where I happened to be located. This wasn't just with Wayne. This occurred with anything that was negative to me. Downplaying—all along that same line of keep saying it's not real and it can't hurt. But I wasn't downplaying what caused the seizure. Not really. What I was downplaying was the fact that it had happened because it hurt. And I wanted to forget about it so that the pain would disappear. "Yeah, Pat," I said finally, "Maybe you're right. In fact, you are right. I'm still upset that this happened, and right now I don't care about why. Not yet. I haven't reached that point."

She shook her head, concerned. "Well, hell, Jodi, how long do you need? To care about why? It's been three weeks already. Have you made an appointment with your neurologist yet?"

"No."

"Why not? Don't you think that's something you ought to do?"

"It's too expensive for me to go see him, Pat. I don't have insurance, and I don't have enough money. Even worse, though, I don't want to see him, especially with the problems I had with the lies he told my mother when I had a grand mal seizure. I just don't want to see somebody that I think is just a quack anyway."

"C'mon. Get over the past. And it doesn't cost that much. Fifty bucks? Sixty? One hundred? You make over one hundred in two days. Why don't you spend your money on what you need instead of letting it be spent on what someone else wants, like Wayne and his liquor? That's

Jodi Sullivan

almost an everyday thing. You'd have the money to see your doctor in two weeks for what he spends of it on alcohol."

The internal wince felt worse than being hit over the head with a two by four. Damn. I sipped on the coffee. I didn't say anything. The pain inside didn't go anywhere. Truth can really hurt sometimes.

44

The opportunity came from nowhere, absolutely nowhere…just like the needles had fallen from out of the ceiling that day, out of nowhere. Dilaudids. Again. And I didn't even need to use the money I'd been hiding for the doctor. I had enough to buy. Just by chance. Just because of a few good days at work. And it was my day off, and it was early, and I'd been sulky—for weeks now. And I remembered the other time I had shot D's. I thought about how it made me leave: leave reality, leave the planet altogether. And while gone, I forgot about the misery of where I was and had been, and I forgot about Wayne. Temptation. What a hell of a temptation to float off into the land of Oblivion. I reached in my purse and grabbed the cash. I bought more than I needed.

This wasn't just my money this time, either. Ricky and Tommy paid up front, paid what they should for a change instead of spending my dollars. They paid their half, then we found ourselves in a predicament when the box was pulled out of the ceiling. We were down to the last needle. Strangely, I wanted to watch. I had always been the first one and had never really known what I might have looked like doped up, so I waited my turn in order to see. The lighter flickered underneath the spoon, and I watched as the liquid separated from the ingredients that tablified the pill. Ricky and Tommy both sprawled out on the floor instantly when their turn came around. I felt the needle, dulled just a little, just enough to make it hurt some, almost more than it should.

The burning sensation spread rapidly up my arm in a straight line, right up a vein that started in the wrist and shot quickly to the brain. For just a second, I wondered. I wondered if this could be the reason. The other time. Could this be why my anticonvulsants for the seizures had been jolted and just didn't work right anymore? Hell, I decided as the world began to fade away, it didn't matter. Not really. There was no way to turn any of the past around to find out. No way to take any of it back. And now there was no way to turn away the burning sensation, no way to take back the Dilaudid and say I had changed my mind. It was in.

When I landed from the high, I looked around, feeling a little disoriented and trying to remember where I was. Looks familiar. Oh yeah. The resting spot on the walk. "How the hell did I get here?" I asked myself out loud.

"I brought you."

I wheeled around. Mike was sitting behind me, just sitting sometimes, then sitting and looking around. He looked disappointed. I felt my heart jump. Oddly, I couldn't talk. I just didn't know what to say. When I finally could muster up a few words, I didn't say much. "Ah, shit," I whispered hoarsely.

Mike didn't move. He just stayed behind me, sitting and looking. "You shot the D's again, huh?"

I looked away. "Yeah."

"Why? And I don't think the reason is boredom."

"Just depressed," I honestly answered, "That last seizure I had has really kept me depressed and I don't know how to get out of this funk."

He slid down the hill and sat beside me. I felt relieved, for just a second. I had thought he was moving on, like hope does, while I'm under the interstate. "Sure." His voice was soft when it touched me. "But what else? It can't just be the seizure that drove you to shoot D's. I know you better than that."

"Last week," I told him, "Last week has really been getting to me, Mike. It's been a year, a whole fucking year since this started."

I could see sadness in his face and deep in his dark eyes, even though he was smiling. "Yeah, and you're still here."

"I know.'

"Still, Jodi."

"I said I know."

He repeated it again. "Still."

"Mike, you're pissing me off."

He laughed, running his warm fingers softly across my back. A year ago that would have made me nervous, but now it had become the affection that I needed, the affection that I was starving for while in the throes of desire. He half shrugged. "I suppose I'm trying to piss you off. Maybe because you don't listen. I keep saying the same thing over and over and over again. Hell, maybe someday you'll hear it. Maybe someday you'll listen."

I sulked. "You think I don't hear what you say?"

He shrugged, still grinning. "Sure you do, babe. Sure you do. You hear. But you don't listen. I keep saying get out of here. And you're still here. And now you've gone and done the D's again. You let Wayne control you. Now you look like you are going to let the drugs control you, too. Ever stop to think about self-control?"

"Mike, come on, it's not that serious. It's only the second time I've ever done it. And you know about both of them."

"But it's again, baby. The first time can be a write off. A mistake you made. That's where you can always use the excuse that you really didn't know what you were doing, what you were getting into. Just like Wayne. The first time he slapped you, it could have been a write off. The second time should have told you what you're really in." I was getting cold. The drug was wearing off and the freezing temperature was absorbing through my coat. Mike continued, "With my brother and now with the D's, you're being dependent. You have allowed yourself to be controlled by other people and now by other things."

Dependent. Damn. He wasn't beating around the bush this time. He wasn't dropping hints. He had just outright said it. In my face he had. "Mike, don't you think that you are being a little tough by saying that? That I would let myself be controlled by other people and things?"

He sighed. "No, babe. I'm not being tough with you. And I'm not being mean or trying to hurt you. I'm just trying to be honest with you by telling you what I can see while I'm

Jodi Sullivan

on the outside looking in." I didn't reply. I just shivered in the cold air. Mike pulled me close. "Kid, I'm sorry. I'm sorry it hurts. But will you think about it, please?" I half smiled to say okay. Mike pulled me to my feet. "Come on, let's go home. It's late."

45

The clock was nearing midnight, almost closing time, and I was glad. This had just been another day that I wanted to pass, just like the holidays. Stressed. Today was a special day, and I was stressed because the day didn't feel special to me. I was pushing away the significance as much as I could. I had been twenty-four for less than twenty-four hours. And it was my year now, the year of the tiger in Chinese astrology. I was just glad my birthday was almost over and no one had noticed. I just let it go by. Just come and go, come and go, like the overhead traffic whizzing by like hope.

The doors were locked. I took a deep breath and sighed. April had stayed after she got off the floor. She had offered me a ride home and was waiting for me. I looked at Debbie and the other workers. "C'mon, let's speed it up. Everybody's gone and we can be out of here in twenty minutes."

I started filling the sugars without noticing anything. I must have been blind. Six people walked out of the kitchen. How did they get there? They were all the workers who had left early. They had entered through the kitchen, along with a cake, all singing happy birthday to me. And I was surprised. Real surprised. I sat down in one of the booths and suddenly laughed. I laughed at how good I felt to be noticed and how easily I had been fooled. So easy. I asked, "How did you guys know it was my birthday? I didn't tell anybody."

April grinned. "We've known for quite a while. We keep up on things around here. You have an employee file just like everyone else does around here. Can't keep a birthday secret. Not here."

The smile felt real, and I wondered why I had hidden this from my fellow employees. I had convinced myself that I just wanted it to pass, just whiz by like the cars overhead on the interstate. This restaurant was a place I liked to be. I always felt good when working or out with April and Debbie. I felt like I didn't have to worry about being me. And I didn't feel so helpless or overwhelmed. And I couldn't figure it out right then, why I had let myself shrink and hide into a shell. Just a shell, like I was doing with

In the Air

Wayne—hiding, running. My world from home was overflowing elsewhere, into the joy, where it shouldn't be.

An hour later, April and I pulled into the driveway. She shut off the headlights before pulling in, and we just sat there in the dark. We both just sat back and listened to the radio. "Listen, Jodi. How long has it been now?"

I flicked ashes out the window. "How long has what been?"

"The abuse."

I stiffened. April was certainly straightforward. I sat for a few minutes, saying nothing. It had been awhile, several months, since we had talked about the abuse and how she could see what I was hiding, right through the makeup. "A year," I said while staring out the window. My voice sounded so soft that it was quiet enough to give me the creeps. "It's been going on now for a year and a few weeks."

April looked straight at me. "I think it's been three or four months since we talked about it that one night."

"Yeah," I agreed. "It's been awhile."

April sighed, then looked away, out at Little Creek Road. "I've left you alone. I don't say much, maybe, but I've seen it since. And now on a day like today, your birthday, I can't help but wonder. Are you going to see twenty-five? Are you still going to be here putting up with this when you turn twenty-six? Are you going to be one who sticks it out for three years? You know, like me?"

I shrugged. "I don't know."

She smiled, looking dreamy and far away. "You know, if I could make a wish come true for your birthday, I would wish that I could make you leave what you're in. To me, that would have been a great birthday present for you. Unfortunately, I couldn't put that wish in a box and wrap it up."

I smiled as the tears welled in my eyes. "Thanks anyway, April. It's a great wish. You didn't need a box for it."

46

I could feel it, like electricity running through me as if I were being electrocuted. The time, the anger wasn't provoked by my sarcasm. Instead, it had risen over the money. Wayne was pissed. I had put aside money to see my doctor, and he hadn't known about it. And he wanted to know why I had been hiding it from him. "Look, I was hiding it from everybody, including myself, so I would have it when I need it. Doctors don't see you for free, you know."

And I sat there in the leather recliner and listened to how much I didn't trust him. "What's your fucking problem?" he demanded, over and over. I didn't answer while I speculated on how many beers and bottles of Jack Daniels that Wayne had gone without since the money had been stashed. I just stared at him while he cursed, speculating about how ugly his face could become and how repulsive he could appear while his face was contorted into a snarl, reddened by his anger. While he ranted, the juggler vein popped out of his neck. How evil he appeared to the eye when he assumed this identity of the monster, the monster from some fairy tale—the one that I was in, wondering what had happened to the happily ever after ending. He asked me again, "Why were you hiding it?"

"Wayne, as far as I'm concerned, that is money that has already been spent. Christ, it's been seven weeks since I had that first seizure, and I should have seen my doctor much sooner than this. But I haven't. And the only reason I haven't gone is I have no insurance, so I have to pay up front and I haven't saved up enough yet to go. So back off, would you?"

He hesitated, but gave me the accusatory stare. "You haven't had any more of those since that day."

The knowing, serious laugh rose into my throat. "Oh yes, I have. Two more. I just haven't told you or anybody else. And there could have been more in my sleep for all I know. Just because you haven't witnessed them doesn't mean that they aren't occurring. I'm the only one with me twenty-four hours a day."

Exasperation had me as I spoke the truth. Two more seizures had happened since my birthday, and both times I had been alone. The first was just a couple days after my birthday and had happened while I sat on the cold concrete

In the Air

under the interstate, listening to the traffic whizzing by, coming and going, coming and going like hope. And my thoughts had been going really fast that time. Far too fast. And when I had come out of the seizure, I was standing on the sidewalk and cars were honking at me as I was right on the curb, ready to step off into the moving traffic. Both of the seizures had come while I thought about other people who knew what was happening; one came while I thought of April, looking dreamy, another when I thought about Pat and her southern drawl and how pissed off she got when she found out I had money to go buy some Jack Daniels but I hadn't been to the doctor yet. Thinking, just thinking too much while the traffic was whizzing by overhead. And now I was doing this all over again. Thinking, thinking hard for just a few seconds while Wayne stood right in front of me. I pushed the thoughts away quickly. I can't think deeply. I can't let myself think deeply with Wayne around and in the midst of an argument.

Wayne's angered distortion of face had vanished, replaced by a sullen, skeptical glance. "How come you didn't tell me about the other two?"

I laughed even though this wasn't funny. "Don't feel left out. I didn't tell anyone. Listen, I need to catch the bus or I'll miss the appointment. The bus runs in about five minutes."

    I grabbed my coat, sighing and thinking what a half assed answer that had been. He would have been the last one to know anyway. Fake. If it was fake. That's all I could think about at the bus stop. If it had been fake, then he was going to beat the shit out of me. Seven weeks ago. Those feelings mixed with the feeling I had when it happened, just like the traffic overhead, coming and going, coming and going, and whizzing by like hope. Wayne didn't understand how much the seizures hurt, not physically, but in my head. Nor did he know how much his words had intensified that pain. He really didn't. And I didn't care anymore to try and explain. I was so far away now, so far from the monster in my fairy tale, just waiting for the story to go away. Keep saying it's not real and it can't hurt. And now I was just waiting, waiting for the bus. It was late already.

47

Again, and it had been too soon. This wasn't much, not compared to the other times. It wasn't like the grip, or the V. This time all I got was an ordinary backhand. Ordinary. At least I had been able to fly along with it. Again. Fly again. And I didn't say a damn thing. Instead, I picked up my purse and just walked out the door, without a word.

And this had been too soon. Wayne hadn't been the same. He had worsened ever since he had found the hidden money that I had put aside to pay the doctor. Worsened. And I kept trying to figure out why, trying to rationalize the irrational. I walked to the drugstore, wondering again, wondering why I was still here. I thought hard while my feet plodded on the frozen sidewalk. I thought about leaving. I thought about this until I couldn't think anymore, until my brain reached overkill.

I came out of the seizure still standing on the sidewalk, thanking God that I hadn't wandered out into the traffic. I'd even kept walking in the right direction, toward the drugstore. I must have been determined to reach my destination this time. And when I did, Pat saw me and was shaking her head at me before I could even sit down. "Again, huh?"

"No shit."

She sighed, flagged down the waitress, and ordered my coffee for me. When it got there, she even fixed it for me, too, by adding two half and half creamers. I grinned, but the grin hurt. I could hear her southern drawl, barely. My head was in a state where everything seemed far away, including me. Pat's voice finally reached me through the sense of distance. "For the longest time, I've figured that you just function on delayed reaction. You know, like you haven't really felt any of this yet. Or like it just hasn't been hard enough yet to sink into that hard head of yours."

I let out a desperate laugh of hope and grief. "It sure would be nice if it couldn't be felt."

Pat sipped on her coffee. And damn, she was staring at me over the top of those reading glasses again. She looked away, quiet for a moment while sipping more of her coffee. Finally, she continued, "But then I realized that I'm being as bad as you are, denying the reality of how serious this really is. Yeah, me, too." She lightly smacked my arm so I would look at her. "Delayed reaction is a copout, Jodi. And I was going along and believing this isn't serious. For a while, anyway."

I set my coffee down. The usual, sarcastic tone wasn't rolling in her drawl. She was talking straight. Delayed reaction. And she had believed my situation wasn't too much. And I already knew that believing is half of anything. "Okay, Pat, so what do I function on then?"

A half laugh answered, the type that comes when there is no humor involved, only truth. "Oh, I'd say it's outright stupidity. Or maybe insanity. Or maybe it's a combination of the two." I stayed quiet. There was no room to argue. "By the way, the welt is pretty close to your eye. You're probably going to end up with a beautiful shiner. So are you just going to cover it up? Again?"

I shrugged. "Why bother? It's not worth the effort."

48

"How long have you been here?"

I watched Mike as he moved towards me, hiking up the concrete hill under the interstate. I inhaled the smoke from the drag off my cigarette as I looked at my watch. Over two hours. "A while," I replied. "I've been here quite a while."

"How long?"

"About two and a half hours."

He sat down beside me and lit a cigarette from mine, then pulled my head around softly and stared, for just a few seconds. "When did this happen? Last night?"

"No. About three and a half hours ago."

He sighed, and a long silence followed, the type I didn't mind. With Mike, the silence always calmed me, unlike silence with Wayne, where I felt threatened by it. Another half hour passed without a word from either one of us. I just listened to the traffic overhead whizzing by, just

In the Air

whizzing by while Mike sat next to me, going nowhere. And I wished the silence could stay forever, too. But I knew it wouldn't. It couldn't. "Damn. Haven't you had enough of this yet? How much more do you need, kid? Where the hell is your breaking point? Can you tell me where it is?"

I stared at the cracks, my head racing in all directions. Cracks. Racing through the concrete. And how many more cracks would it take to just make the concrete crumble, crumble down to dust? And how many more cracks existed? Not in the concrete. How many more cracks existed in me? I'd felt cracks enough. And this was a good question, what Mike asked. Where was it? Where was my breaking point? "I don't know where it is, Mike."

For a few seconds, he looked lost, as if he were looking for the right words to say and just couldn't find them. And a look of desperation swept over him for just a flash, like he was letting himself feel the pain—the same pain that I was in. Or maybe the pain he was feeling came from somewhere else, from those years that I didn't know about. Maybe these were the ones that he had buried a long time ago, even from himself. Yeah, that could be what it was all right. I'm not sure how many times Mike had pointed out to me that Wayne had been my lover for two years (three now!), but Wayne had been his older brother all his life.

Mike's face eventually relaxed. The words finally came. "You seem so determined. You just seem so determined to make sure you know exactly where your breaking point is. I'm starting to wonder if you even have one."

I laughed. And this felt weird, real weird, like the roles had been reversed and, in that instant, I was the one soothing him and trying to make it all better. Yeah, there sure were a lot of years that I didn't know about. "Mike, I promise you I'm not on a masochistic search for my breaking point. I'm not looking for the snap."

He put his hand on my shoulder, making sure my eyes were looking into his. "Then get the hell out of here. Get out before you do find it. You get closer every day."

49

The next day, I got lost in my head. My thoughts wandered aimlessly. Christ, and that was all in a conscious state rather than in a seizure. I stared at my medicine bottle. The dosage had been upped a little. And it had been a few weeks now, and I hadn't had any more seizures since the dosage change was stabilized. Yet something about this was bothering me, and I was in a state of confusion, groping. For what, I didn't know. I just wanted an answer. I just wanted to know why I was feeling so troubled all of a sudden. Once the dosage had been increased, the seizures had stopped, and it had been a little more than three weeks since the last seizure had occurred. I should have been feeling great, happy that the seizures were back under control. Life was so much better without them. But while I stared at the medicine bottle, all I felt was pissed off, like the snowcap was fixing to fly right off of the volcano within me. And I just couldn't figure out why I was having such a strange feeling when everything was going the way it should, as if there were a sharp wire hair stuck up my ass.

I kept staring at the medicine bottle, and suddenly I knew why, I just knew. For three weeks, I had been seizure free. But really, it should have been longer than that. In fact, it should have been closer to ten weeks, closer to when the first one had happened. But continual alcohol for Wayne and Dilaudids for changing my mood had come first, chosen as a priorities before the drugs I really needed for survival, for my own health, to prevent the seizures which I couldn't handle on my own.

The other two that had happened on the concrete hill flashed through my head along with the one that had occurred on my walk to the drugstore. Those might not have existed if I had gone to the doctor sooner, much sooner, like I should have. I swallowed the pills, understanding why I was pissed. I was just mad at me right then. My priorities had sucked worse than ever before. And I thought even harder. If I really care that little about myself, I must be getting closer to my breaking point, closer than I think.

50

April 1st was April Fools' Day, and I wondered right then how much of a fool I was, a real one and not just a quick slapstick victim of a jokester. I decided that pretty quickly. Without having to really weigh the pros and cons, since the cons were the only options, the answer was easy, too easy, and a true scare.

I waited that night for Wayne to fall asleep. I was edgy. I wanted to take a walk. I hadn't had enough of those lately and I needed one. The wait felt like eternity, the longest ten minutes I had ever gone through. Finally, Wayne's soft snore drifted into the air, and I breathed a sigh of relief. I waited a few more minutes, just to let his sleep get a little deeper, then I slipped through the front door and out into the cool night air. Mike and Ricky were out in the yard, smoking a joint. I smiled. "Hey, guys."

They finished toking on the joint, and Mike stopped me as I stepped into the road. "Where are you going this late?"

I stared at him a second, wondering if he had lost his mind, but then I realized he was just playing stupid, like he didn't know. A smart move on April Fools' Day. "I'm just not tired. I'm hyper. I thought I would go take a long walk around the block to burn off some of this energy so I can crash."

Mike suggested, "Let me come with you, then. You shouldn't be out there alone." And then to really make it look authentic, he turned and asked, "Want to come along with us, Ricky?"

Ricky shook his head. "No, man. I need to get home."

After we walked far enough down the road and away from the house, Mike asked, "What's bothering you?"

I shrugged. "Nothing, really."

"You're edgy," he pointed out. "Did you argue with Wayne?"

"No. Thank God. It's just the day that's got me. April Fools'." And I told Mike how I had been going through this for the entire year. Mind games always came to visit me on holidays. Thanksgiving through Christmas has really been hell. The season to be jolly. Right. That had been a real screwer for my head. Holidays. How exhausting.

Mike nodded when I finished. "That ought to tell you something, kid. That really ought to tell you a lot." We were sitting in the grass. The air was cold, but it wasn't freezing. "Holidays aren't supposed to be exhausting. In fact, they're supposed to do the opposite of that. You know, give you a lift in spirits."

I sighed. "A lift, huh?" I looked at Mike and smiled, wondering right then where his wings were. Angel wings. "Well, Mike, there's been a lot of times that I've had some lifts in my spirit, too, in the last year."

"When?"

I felt the grin. "Any time you give me a hug. That's been more of a lift than any holiday has been." He wrapped his arms around me, and the hug lasted for a long time. It sure didn't feel like it was a foolish thing to do. And it was past midnight now anyway.

51

At work, April and I sat in the back room while on break together. I stared at the spaghetti on the plate, twirling it in my fork, wondering what the hell was wrong. Six days had gone by since I had actually eaten anything. I had tried every day to eat something, then almost as soon as I started, I felt full and just stopped. Way too soon, I felt full, nearly stuffed after four to five bites. In fact, I felt so stuffed that it was like I had overeaten when I had hardly put anything in my mouth.

April kept eating slowly and watching me. "Jodi, come on and eat some more before it gets cold on you."

I shrugged, not really sure how to explain this to her when I didn't really understand it myself. "I don't know what's going on," I told her. "I'm full, April—on five bites."

"Something is wrong with you," she determined as she bit into her own spaghetti. "You haven't really eaten anything for a week. You haven't even been drinking much, either. And you're starting to look like shit."

"Gee, thanks for the compliment."

"Hell, it's just a fact."

After work, April offered me a ride and we went to the all night diner because I was feeling slightly hungry. This seemed like a good sign. And a cheeseburger sounded really good to me—medium rare with French fries. But while we waited, just the smell of the food started to shut down the hunger. After a few fries and three bites of the burger, I was already full. April sighed. "Jodi, something is wrong with you. You need to go see a doctor. Have you lost weight?"

"Yeah," I admitted. "I've dropped ten pounds from 110 to 100 in the last week."

She sat back in the booth and took a long look at me. "Christ. Promise me you'll go see your doctor. I'm worried."

"Yeah. I guess I got to go."

The next morning, I was dead asleep. I could hear the phone ringing in the pitch black dark of the attic bedroom, and I jumped up out of the bed to answer it. And I fell right on my face, never balanced. I was dizzy. And suddenly, I was scared, even more than April had sounded the night before. Frightened because this was me. This was my body. I had no control over my life, and now I had no control over my body, either. I tried to stand up again but couldn't escape the spinning sensation in my head, so I fell onto the bed. This had to be it. This had to be death.

Within the first hour, the itch attacked me all over. No balance, and now I was covered with an itch. Just more out of control. Insane. This was insane. And it was driving me crazy while I couldn't decide where to scratch next. I didn't have enough hands or nails to reach all the spots at once, so I tried to focus on the most intense spots, which was hard to do because they all seemed strong. I just kept digging into my skin, clawing at the itch.

Finally, I was staring at a doctor in the emergency room. He scowled down at me. "So, do you shoot drugs?"

"No," I lied.

"Well, kid," he stated matter-of-factly, "You have hepatitis, the type that comes from shooting drugs. You're going to be sick for quite a while, for a couple of months. Usually, this lasts for about six to eight weeks. Do you know anybody else that shoots drugs?"

I broke down. "Yes."

He stared at me. I could tell he was trying to filter through my answers and figure out my lies. He was quiet for a long time, then finally he said, "Well, this is a contagious disease. It's not easy to pass on other than through the blood, but it's remotely possible to pick up other ways besides a needle."

Two times. Damn. I had only shot the D's two times and only used a dirty needle once. And I had what some junkies never get. How much more unlucky could I get? I spent nine days in the hospital, and the first few days felt close to death. Two times. And I just wanted to stay in the hospital. With the information about the six to eight weeks, I knew I wouldn't be able to work. As I gazed out of the hospital window, I felt trapped, like a tiger in a cage, pacing furiously back and forth, back and forth, and aching to be set free in the wild.

52

I was glad to be out, even though I was still brooding at the same time. Hospitals drive me crazy and I was out. I had no energy, and I just sat listless in the leather chair. I just sat, trying hard, really hard. I wouldn't be able to work for at least another five weeks and not until cleared by a doctor. That would be somewhere in the middle of June. And I was going through what I had experienced before, when I had the grand mal seizure—the state of mind that had taken forever to get rid of, the constant dread in a state of fear and paralysis.

My dread in the presence of Wayne seemed magnified, even worse than it had ever felt before. I didn't have my job to escape to, to rely on as an easy out. According to the doctors, I was supposed to stay home, and supposed to rest. So I sat in the chair, trying to figure out how to do what the doctors ordered while living with a monster from some fairy tale. And now I was seeing how much of a break I had really had. Until this moment.

And Wayne knew this. He knew. He was using my state to his advantage, and using it well for manipulation. He capitalized on regaining the control that he had been missing for a while. Not getting enough of it, I guess. The first day I was home, he wouldn't let me take a walk. And now it was the next day, and I was trying to get out for a while, just to escape for a few minutes. "You are supposed to be taking it easy," he argued when I said I was going to go for a walk.

I sighed and snapped, "Jesus Christ. I'm just sick, Wayne. But I'm not an invalid, and I don't want to be treated like one."

He kept arguing with me. "The doctors said you need to get rest. What do you need to go on a walk for?" I didn't want to argue. I was too sick to argue but not too sick to move, and I just wanted to take a walk. But I was too weak to be assertive, to push by Wayne and just leave like I had in the past. As the arguing continued, the volume rose, like blaring music up too loud. But it was just coming from his side, not mine. I tried to yell back, but I couldn't. I just kept talking softly because that's all that I could do. And I kept watching him change form, right into the monster, the one from my fairy tale, with his face contorted like an angry ogre. And he just got angrier and uglier, until he exploded like a bomb and until I couldn't see anymore. I couldn't see for just a few seconds, as I flew, again, across the room, a few feet, stopped by the wall. Again, just like the first time.

    Maybe it was the wall, the jolt of the wall as I came to a dead stop. Right then, I felt my words turn around in my head. The words I had just said. I wasn't an invalid, but I sure was sick. And this was no fairy tale. And Wayne was no monster—just a man. Half crazy, maybe, but just a man. And this was real. And it hurt. And all the cracks inside cracked just a little more. And I pictured myself like the concrete hill, under the interstate where the traffic keeps whizzing by overhead. Like hope. And I was just crumbling, just like the concrete does once the cracks reach a certain point, a breaking point. So it was here, the breaking point—my breaking point. And as far as I was concerned, I believed this fairy tale was over. And believing is half of anything. So I decided that this one was going to end happily ever after, even if it killed me to get there.

53

I was at the airport, caught in a high. Thank God for family, bailing me out. I had stood at the payphone, calling collect. My mother had accepted the call. Through the sobs, I begged, "Mom, get me out of here. Please."

I already had a ticket waiting for me at the airport. After my mother had already bought the plane ticket, I found Pat, and she drove me to the airport, the whole time caught up in a state of rejoicing and saying "Hallelujah!" over and over again. Even though I had to wait all night, that didn't matter. That didn't matter to me at all. I waited while in the biggest high I had ever felt. Away. Gone. And further up than any plane was ever going to take me.

My left eye had swelled shut. I had to go back to get a few things, vital necessities, like my medication. What I was doing was obvious. And this argument was the longest and its price the heaviest, but now it was over, and I laid in the airport, breathing deeply. My head wasn't under the water anymore. I gulped all the free air I wanted. This was all under my control, finally. The air was free and I was in it, just as free.

When the plane lifted from the runway, I lifted off, too, heading for Miami, eleven hundred miles away. I looked at the clouds through the airplane window, realizing I was doing what everybody had been telling me to do for a long time. Mike's "Get out of here." April's wish. Pat's advice on heading to Jamaica and that time she had told me she had saved money for an airplane ticket. They would all still be living in Norfolk and in separate worlds. They would all be feeling the same way, too—happy that I was finally gone.

In the air. I was in the air, moving smooth, flying free, and letting go of a life gone by. In the air, flying now to another world, where I prayed I wouldn't end up on another, different concrete hill, where the traffic whizzes by overhead. Like hope. I was in the air, and I never would have cared if the plane had stayed there for the rest of my life.

54

The temperature was 98 degrees with just about as much humidity. This was August, with the heat enough to kill anyone, including me. But I needed the walk. The phone call had been a week earlier. Wayne had found the information about my grandparents in Miami in an old telephone pad I had left behind. And now there was a letter from him, asking for my forgiveness.

I should have known, should have foreseen that this was going to happen. Everything I owned was eleven hundred miles away, back in Norfolk, back up north and left behind—including address books. And now I felt like a foreign person in a foreign land. Even though I had grown up in Miami, it wasn't the same because I had changed. I felt like a stranger even though I was home.

Beads of sweat rolled down the back of my neck, and down my forehead, into my eye, blinding me with the salty wetness. Blinking, I stared at the concrete hill, in Miami

Jodi Sullivan

under the Palmetto Expressway, where I had played as a kid, hiding from adults and smoking cigarettes. Yet it looked oddly more familiar than that. Too familiar. I climbed up the concrete and sat underneath, listening to the traffic overhead, whizzing by. Like time. That's all it sounded like now, like time ticking away.

Caught, I was, trapped in my own head. Still. Wayne was far away from me now, but it was just as easy to feel and to hurt and to forget, just forget the last year and a half. And remember instead the year and a half to two years before that when times had just been fun. And believe again, believe this could all be pieced back together like a jigsaw puzzle. With the use of over-rationalizing, and over-simplification, I figured that this was a problem and all problems have solutions. Infinite words. I was believing them, and believing is half of anything. I was doing just that while under the expressway, along with the traffic whizzing by overhead. Like time. And driving me crazy, making me wonder where my sense was because I believed something I knew I shouldn't.

Even in the shade, the air was so hot that it made me sweat. And for just a minute, I hoped. I prayed that I wouldn't be stupid. I hoped that I would listen to my head screaming no and not my heart that was coming up with excuses. The fairy tale was over. Finished. Three months ago. Wasn't it? I sighed, stepping back into the brutal sunlight, heading home, wishing that the feeling of loneliness would fry right through my skin and pour itself out in sweat. And I heard the wish, the one for sanity, out on the expressway, whizzing by.

55

Most of my family were pissed the day Wayne arrived in Miami, and they made sure I knew that, real well, but then this was completely dropped as if the bail out had never happened, like it didn't really matter. I was an adult, and this was my life, so it was my decision to make. And the air came along with that choice, the air of indifference that comes when people give up or get frustrated.

The only exception to this was my grandfather. He didn't have that air of indifference. I'm not sure what his mood was, really, but my grandmother years later said that he was nothing but petrified. In the moment, though, I didn't know what he was feeling, just that he didn't seem like himself. Then Wayne's rifle turned up missing from the stuff he had packed in the back of his pickup truck. The bed of the truck was full of belongings from Virginia, and nothing else was missing but the rifle. I asked my

In the Air

grandfather if he had any idea where the rifle had gone. And he just said, real quiet, "No one needs a damn gun."

As frustrated as I felt, I felt good, too. And it was strange to feel such opposing feelings at the same time. I could tell by how he wouldn't look at me that he knew where the gun was, all right. He had done something with it. And for nobody else but me. "Where is it, Papa?"

He lit a cigarette and blew the smoke absently into the air. And his voice stayed the same—quiet, matter-of-fact, eerily calm. He shrugged. "Doesn't matter where it is. Like I said, nobody needs a gun. And some need them less than others."

After a full week of everyone hounding him to give back what wasn't his to take, he finally gave in and told my grandmother where it was—broken down into parts and hidden in three different places inside the house. One piece was in an overhead storage area while another was in the attic. The third was packed in an old, beat up suitcase in the hall closet. And every piece had been carefully wrapped up so it couldn't be seen or noticed easily.

Once put back together, I stared at the gun leaning in the corner of the bare living room in the apartment Wayne and I had rented. As I gazed at it, back in one piece, I could still hear my grandfather's voice, quiet, just telling me

Jodi Sullivan

matter-of-factly. Like it's easy. Like it's something that everybody ought to know. And few do. Just a statement—nobody needs a damn gun. All said to nobody else except me. His voice, so far away from everyone else in the family, who all just sounded indifferent, acting like what I was going through, good or bad, just wasn't their business.

56

At my job, we worked on a split shift. The breaks between lunch and dinner were long, sometimes three to four hours. And the restaurant, named Shorty's, was only a little more than half a mile from the concrete hill under the expressway. That was walking distance. And I found myself caught in a ritual of using the walk and the hill to escape, to think, and to try and figure out what was feeling so wrong when everything seemed to be going so right. The outcome seemed to be just like what I wanted. Like the first year and a half. Like the mean ogre had transformed into my Prince Charming. And the pieces of the puzzle had fit back together nicely, just like when times had been fun.

And now it had been over a month, already the end of September. Wayne had a job. What a change. This sure was different. Everything had changed, just into what I wanted. The new location was eleven hundred miles away. Wayne was working and actually making efforts to go out of his way for a change. I could tell. He made efforts to do things for me, silly things like opening the door for me. That was new altogether. That had never existed before, not even in the good times. Not to this degree, to where it could be noticed. And no alcohol, either. Not a drop. Not with my money, and not with his own, either.

Everything was just perfect, or so it seemed. I had been given exactly what I had believed I really wanted and hoped for, all like making a wish while throwing a penny in magic waters and having it come true. I had precisely what I had thought I wanted, exactly, to the tee—and perfect. And I sat on the concrete hill under the expressway, trying to figure me out, trying to make sense out of why I was feeling troubled when my wishes had come true, like a dream—just like a dream.

The traffic whizzed by overhead. And that's all it sounded like—like traffic overhead whizzing by. And I sat motionless on the hill, listening for feelings. And none came. Right then, I realized that feelings were probably eleven hundred miles away, on another concrete hill under an interstate where the traffic whizzes by overhead. Like hope. But here, under the expressway, feelings were just thoughts now, nothing more.

In the Air

I reflected back to the one day in August that I sat here, overwhelmed. Weren't those feelings real? Not really, I thought, because my mind had travelled that day, and so had my heart. They had travelled in the air eleven hundred miles away to the other concrete hill, where the feelings were probably dead and buried. Deep. Real deep in the cracks that I had left behind.

So I had pieced everything back together, back to when times had been fun, and it all seemed perfect. Too perfect—like a dream. And I kept listening to the traffic while it talked to me, just sounding like what it really was—traffic. And I struggled real hard and for a real long time to feel love. But I didn't.

57

Asleep, I was far away in some dream, a real dream, and I was jolted awake by the telephone. I reached for it and knocked it off the nightstand while groping for it. The clock stared back at me, showing one in the morning. Who the hell was calling me and waking me up at one in the morning?

My mother was on the other end, telling me, letting me know, using the type of words that no one ever wants to hear, no one ever wants to believe. My grandfather had lung cancer still in the early stages, so nobody worried too much. He had gotten up to go to the bathroom, and, while there, an artery had ruptured on his lung. He had died instantly. The paramedics said he was probably gone before he even hit the tile floor. At least it was fast instead of the long suffering that everyone had already braced for.

I felt like asking her what made her think she knew this was all so easy. Had she been there inside his head? Did

In the Air

she know what he was thinking while it happened? It might have seemed like forever to him.

And all I could think about the next few days was his voice. I was going through the routine of a viewing, of a funeral. For me, this was the first true experience of losing someone close to me. I had spent nine years of my childhood with my grandparents and was closest to Papa, who had always taken me to watch airplanes take off at Miami's International Airport or on fishing trips in the Keys. And now it was all coming back, the importance of time, of those nine years and what they meant to me, then and now.

As the casket closed, I walked away, feeling removed. Others from his family had fallen on the casket, sobbing but I had kept my distance because he was gone. But I was still listening to him. I still heard his voice, hearing what he had told me just a few weeks ago. Christ, time is short. "No one needs a gun." So quiet. So calm. So matter-of-fact. Just a simple statement. That's all that had been then. Just a statement. But it had something in it that no one else in the family seemed to have—it had feelings, and a lot of them. And now he was gone. But I could still feel his words flowing through me. I could hear them quietly whisper into my ears, like a song, the type of song that

Jodi Sullivan

doesn't get forgotten, at least not by the ones who listen to the music.

58

Family from the other side, Wayne's side. After Papa died, Wayne's mother had called him, saying that, since he wasn't there to take care of anything anymore, she wanted to sell the house. She said that he and Mike could have half the money from the house if they fixed it up and sold it. Money. What a temptation that is and always can be for anybody.

And that was fine with me. This would give me a stall for time, the time I was needing to figure out how to get the hell out of this—this perfect relationship. As good as everything seemed, there was something missing now, the most important factor, the one needed to make it last forever—love. That one need had slipped down some crack under some interstate someday up in Virginia. And I wasn't even sure when that had actually happened. I just knew that it was eleven hundred miles away, and it had died there.

I kept spending my long breaks in the same spot, under the expressway and on the concrete hill, trying to rationalize why I felt so cold now and why I had changed. Why was this so real now? This didn't hurt me. I didn't feel any pangs of remorse at all. Not at all, even though it was real because it was what I truly felt. Just cold. Empty. Didn't care anymore. And didn't love anymore. That's what was real now—I was cold, hard, and empty.

    I spent six weeks alone, stuck in my head, engulfed by whom I had become, and wrapped up in what I couldn't seem to get a grasp on. Empty. Cold. Hard. Like I didn't have any say in becoming this way. I didn't just wake up one day and choose this self. It just was. And at first, since believing is half of anything, I tried to believe that this was just a passing phase that I was caught up in. But as each day passed, I doubted this false hope even more and believed it less because I was feeling nothing, nothing at all, except what I had feared I would feel one day when I sat on a concrete hill under an interstate, afraid that I would be cold and hard one day. And I was just that now—cold and hard. Like steel covered by snow—the type that never melts.

    I picked up the phone. Wayne was on the other end, talking about money and buying a boat with it. Excited. He sounded excited, long distance and all. And I sat there, fiddling with the phone cord, knowing, just knowing right then that I wanted to keep everything that way—long distance. "Listen, Wayne, I don't want to get back together. Why don't you just stay up there and I'll stay down here?"

Disbelief and the hesitation that comes with it—a silence that hangs heavy, real heavy, even when it's long distance. And it stayed there longer than it should before he asked me, "Why?"

I sighed. It was only two weeks before Christmas. Guess I was the doer now, doing what had been done to me last year—mind games during the holidays. But this wasn't a game to me anymore. This was real to me because it was the truth. "Wayne, I don't love you anymore."

Silence again. And it was heavy again. And followed by, "Why?" again.

"I just don't."

"Can't you tell me why?"

And I thought of Mike, my angel, whom I had made love to once and who carried me on his wings when I needed to be carried. "I just don't, Wayne. If you really can't figure out why, ask your brother. Ask Mike. He'll tell you why."

"What does Mike have to do with it?"

"Ask him." My voice was cold. "He'll tell you."

I hung up the phone, suddenly pissed at myself, but I didn't know why. I pictured Mike telling Wayne the truth—that he had told me to leave a long time ago. Maybe Mike

Jodi Sullivan

wouldn't tell him that, though. That might piss Wayne off and Wayne had been his older brother all his life. Maybe I had said too much. Ah, hell. Just a maybe. Maybe any innuendos went right over his head. And by the time I went to sleep, I had myself convinced that he had missed it all.

59

Four days later, I was in the midst of a lunch rush, serving ribs and chicken specials for lunch when the phone call came. It didn't even dawn on me that it was long distance on a weekday afternoon. On the other end was Debbie, Mike and Wayne's sister. And she was asking me if Wayne and I had broken up. "Yeah," I said, "We broke up four days ago."

"Well, Mike and Wayne got into an argument last night."

I was perturbed, wondering why she had to be calling me at work to tell me this while I was busy. "So? What else is new?"

"Mike got beat pretty bad, Jodi. He's in the hospital."

Ah, shit. My message didn't go over Wayne's head, like I hoped. Guilt started to set in. "I'm sorry to hear that," I said sincerely.

"And he took the rifle and shot Wayne."

"Sorry to hear that, too. How is he?"

"Jodi, he's dead."

The phone flew from my hand, the receiver moving back like a cobra after a strike, coiling away from me. I screamed. I don't know how I looked. Everyone I worked with was suddenly next to me, asking me what was wrong and holding me up, just holding me. I couldn't see straight. I couldn't see anything, except the phone cord slithering away in my head. The cord that I had played with four days earlier while talking to Wayne on the phone long distance flashed in my head, from when my voice was cold and hard. And when I had wondered for an instant if I had said too much. I stood there, unable to hear what anyone was saying to me, feeling like I was a particle of dust being sucked up through the hose of a giant Hoover vacuum cleaner, running on high.

The power of words. Jesus Christ, the power of words. I had never believed that saying before, not before this, but at this point that was all I could hear over and over in my head. I could hear what I had said four nights ago suddenly echoing in my inner ear, just like the echo of a gunshot. "Ask Mike. He'll tell you why." I had never believed in the power of words. Not before this. And believing is half of anything, including life and death.

60

Right then, I left my mind. And I was out there somewhere—in the air, floating, drifting, and soaring high. The sensation was powerful, stronger than any drug I had ever tried. And I stayed out there, outside of me, for a long time. I couldn't even feel my feet touch the ground when I took my little five year old cousin shopping for Christmas. I walked through nearly a month in an altered state to where I started to believe I would never leave. I thought I was destined to stay there. Forever. Like a bird in flight without a tree to build a nest in for a resting spot—what any animal needs. For peace, peace of mind.

And once I could finally feel my feet on the ground again, at first I was relieved, thinking that I hadn't completely lost my mind after all. And once I started to relax, one day while I was walking to work and trudging up US1, I decided to confront in my head everything that had happened. I stopped cold on the sidewalk, keenly aware of

Jodi Sullivan

my thoughts and how empty they had become. A strange chill shot through me as I became aware that the three years were completely gone, like someone had come along and erased the chalkboard of my memory. Right then, all those memories were out of my reach, out there somewhere in the air, floating freely on their own and separated from me.

Epilogue

The Tiger

The words of death
In silent breath
Echo in my ear.
Listen, child,
They say so mild,
And you will know no fear.
The time is here,
It's been your year,
The tiger in your soul.
It's time to take
The pains that ache
And make the tiger whole.
I hear the calling,
Feel like falling
Away from all this pain.
Make excuses,
Nervous breakdown,
Find someone to blame.

Jodi Sullivan

But the voice says no,

You cannot go,

You've got too much to see.

Too many places

You haven't been,

And a lot you want to be.

The tiger's grown,

And not alone,

So set the tiger free.

    December 17, 1986—two days later

www.ingramcontent.com/pod-product-compliance
Lightning Source LLC
Chambersburg PA
CBHW070602300426
44113CB00010B/1369